SAS® 9.2 SQL Procedure
User's Guide

SAS® Documentation

The correct bibliographic citation for this manual is as follows: SAS Institute Inc., *SAS® 9.2 SQL Procedure User's Guide*. Cary, NC: SAS Institute Inc., 2009.

SAS® 9.2 SQL Procedure User's Guide

Copyright © 2009, SAS Institute Inc., Cary, NC, USA.

ISBN 978–1–599944–853–9

Contents

Chapter 1 △ Introduction to the SQL Procedure   1

What Is SQL?   **1**

What Is the SQL Procedure?   **1**

Terminology   **2**

Comparing PROC SQL with the SAS DATA Step   **3**

Notes about the Example Tables   **5**

Chapter 2 △ Retrieving Data from a Single Table   11

Overview of the SELECT Statement   **12**

Selecting Columns in a Table   **14**

Creating New Columns   **18**

Sorting Data   **25**

Retrieving Rows That Satisfy a Condition   **31**

Summarizing Data   **40**

Grouping Data   **47**

Filtering Grouped Data   **51**

Validating a Query   **53**

Chapter 3 △ Retrieving Data from Multiple Tables   55

Introduction   **56**

Selecting Data from More Than One Table by Using Joins   **56**

Using Subqueries to Select Data   **74**

When to Use Joins and Subqueries   **80**

Combining Queries with Set Operators   **81**

Chapter 4 △ Creating and Updating Tables and Views   89

Introduction   **90**

Creating Tables   **90**

Inserting Rows into Tables   **93**

Updating Data Values in a Table   **96**

Deleting Rows   **98**

Altering Columns   **99**

Creating an Index   **102**

Deleting a Table   **103**

Using SQL Procedure Tables in SAS Software   **103**

Creating and Using Integrity Constraints in a Table   **103**

Creating and Using PROC SQL Views   **106**

Chapter 5 △ Programming with the SQL Procedure   111

Introduction   **112**

Using PROC SQL Options to Create and Debug Queries   **112**

Improving Query Performance   **116**

Accessing SAS System Information by Using DICTIONARY Tables   **120**
Using SAS Data Set Options with PROC SQL   **127**
Using PROC SQL with the SAS Macro Facility   **128**
Formatting PROC SQL Output by Using the REPORT Procedure   **136**
Accessing a DBMS with SAS/ACCESS Software   **137**
Using the Output Delivery System with PROC SQL   **142**

Chapter 6 △ Practical Problem-Solving with PROC SQL   145
Overview   **146**
Computing a Weighted Average   **146**
Comparing Tables   **148**
Overlaying Missing Data Values   **150**
Computing Percentages within Subtotals   **152**
Counting Duplicate Rows in a Table   **153**
Expanding Hierarchical Data in a Table   **155**
Summarizing Data in Multiple Columns   **157**
Creating a Summary Report   **158**
Creating a Customized Sort Order   **161**
Conditionally Updating a Table   **163**
Updating a Table with Values from Another Table   **165**
Creating and Using Macro Variables   **167**
Using PROC SQL Tables in Other SAS Procedures   **170**

Appendix 1 △ Recommended Reading   175
Recommended Reading   **175**

Glossary   177

Index   181

CHAPTER

1

Introduction to the SQL Procedure

What Is SQL? **1**
What Is the SQL Procedure? **1**
Terminology **2**
    Tables **2**
    Queries **2**
    Views **3**
    Null Values **3**
Comparing PROC SQL with the SAS DATA Step **3**
Notes about the Example Tables **5**

What Is SQL?

Structured Query Language (SQL) is a standardized, widely used language that retrieves and updates data in relational tables and databases.

A *relation* is a mathematical concept that is similar to the mathematical concept of a set. Relations are represented physically as two-dimensional tables that are arranged in rows and columns. Relational theory was developed by E. F. Codd, an IBM researcher, and first implemented at IBM in a prototype called System R. This prototype evolved into commercial IBM products based on SQL. The Structured Query Language is now in the public domain and is part of many vendors' products.

What Is the SQL Procedure?

The SQL procedure is the Base SAS implementation of Structured Query Language. PROC SQL is part of Base SAS software, and you can use it with any SAS data set (table). Often, PROC SQL can be an alternative to other SAS procedures or the DATA step. You can use SAS language elements such as global statements, data set options, functions, informats, and formats with PROC SQL just as you can with other SAS procedures. PROC SQL can

- generate reports
- generate summary statistics
- retrieve data from tables or views
- combine data from tables or views
- create tables, views, and indexes
- update the data values in PROC SQL tables
- update and retrieve data from database management system (DBMS) tables

□ modify a PROC SQL table by adding, modifying, or dropping columns.

PROC SQL can be used in an interactive SAS session or within batch programs, and it can include global statements, such as TITLE and OPTIONS.

Terminology

Tables

A PROC SQL *table* is the same as a SAS data file. It is a SAS file of type DATA. PROC SQL tables consist of rows and columns. The rows correspond to observations in SAS data files, and the columns correspond to variables. The following table lists equivalent terms that are used in SQL, SAS, and traditional data processing.

SQL Term	SAS Term	Data Processing Term
table	SAS data file	file
row	observation	record
column	variable	field

You can create and modify tables by using the SAS DATA step, or by using the PROC SQL statements that are described in Chapter 4, "Creating and Updating Tables and Views," on page 89. Other SAS procedures and the DATA step can read and update tables that are created with PROC SQL.

SAS data files can have a one-level name or a two-level name. Typically, the names of temporary SAS data files have only one level, and the data files are stored in the WORK library. PROC SQL assumes that SAS data files that are specified with a one-level name are to be read from or written to the WORK library, unless you specify a USER library. You can assign a USER library with a LIBNAME statement or with the SAS system option USER=. For more information about how to work with SAS data files and libraries, see "Temporary and Permanent SAS Data Sets" in the *Base SAS Procedures Guide*.

DBMS tables are tables that were created with other software vendors' database management systems. PROC SQL can connect to, update, and modify DBMS tables, with some restrictions. For more information, see "Accessing a DBMS with SAS/ ACCESS Software" on page 137.

Queries

Queries retrieve data from a table, view, or DBMS. A query returns a *query result*, which consists of rows and columns from a table. With PROC SQL, you use a SELECT statement and its subordinate clauses to form a query. Chapter 2, "Retrieving Data from a Single Table," on page 11 describes how to build a query.

Views

PROC SQL views do not actually contain data as tables do. Rather, a PROC SQL view contains a stored SELECT statement or query. The query executes when you use the view in a SAS procedure or DATA step. When a view executes, it displays data that is derived from existing tables, from other views, or from SAS/ACCESS views. Other SAS procedures and the DATA step can use a PROC SQL view as they would any SAS data file. For more information about views, see Chapter 4, "Creating and Updating Tables and Views," on page 89.

Note: When you process PROC SQL views between a client and a server, getting the correct results depends on the compatibility between the client and server architecture. For more information, see "Accessing a SAS View" in the *SAS/CONNECT User's Guide.* △

Null Values

According to the ANSI Standard for SQL, a missing value is called a *null value*. It is not the same as a blank or zero value. However, to be compatible with the rest of SAS, PROC SQL treats missing values the same as blanks or zero values, and considers all three to be null values. This important concept comes up in several places in this document.

Comparing PROC SQL with the SAS DATA Step

PROC SQL can perform some of the operations that are provided by the DATA step and the PRINT, SORT, and SUMMARY procedures. The following query displays the total population of all the large countries (countries with population greater than 1 million) on each continent.

```
proc sql;
   title 'Population of Large Countries Grouped by Continent';
   select Continent, sum(Population) as TotPop format=comma15.
      from sql.countries
      where Population gt 1000000
      group by Continent
      order by TotPop;
quit;
```

Output 1.1   Sample SQL Output

```
                    Population of Large Countries Grouped by Continent

                    Continent                               TotPop
                    ------------------------------------------------
                    Oceania                              3,422,548
                    Australia                           18,255,944
                    Central America and Caribbean       65,283,910
                    South America                      316,303,397
                    North America                      384,801,818
                    Africa                             706,611,183
                    Europe                             811,680,062
                    Asia                             3,379,469,458
```

Here is a SAS program that produces the same result.

```
title 'Large Countries Grouped by Continent';
proc summary data=sql.countries;
   where Population > 1000000;
   class Continent;
   var Population;
   output out=sumPop sum=TotPop;
run;

proc sort data=SumPop;
   by totPop;
run;

proc print data=SumPop noobs;
   var Continent TotPop;
   format TotPop comma15.;
   where _type_=1;
run;
```

Output 1.2   Sample DATA Step Output

```
                       Large Countries Grouped by Continent

                    Continent                               TotPop

                    Oceania                              3,422,548
                    Australia                           18,255,944
                    Central America and Caribbean       65,283,910
                    South America                      316,303,397
                    North America                      384,801,818
                    Africa                             706,611,183
                    Europe                             811,680,062
                    Asia                             3,379,469,458
```

This example shows that PROC SQL can achieve the same results as Base SAS software but often with fewer and shorter statements. The SELECT statement that is shown in this example performs summation, grouping, sorting, and row selection. It also displays the query's results without the PRINT procedure.

PROC SQL executes without using the RUN statement. After you invoke PROC SQL you can submit additional SQL procedure statements without submitting the PROC statement again. Use the QUIT statement to terminate the procedure.

Notes about the Example Tables

For all examples, the following global statements are in effect:

```
options nodate nonumber linesize=80 pagesize=60;
libname sql 'SAS-data-library';
```

The tables that are used in this document contain geographic and demographic data. The data is intended to be used for the PROC SQL code examples only; it is not necessarily up-to-date or accurate.

Note: You can find instructions for downloading these data sets at http://ftp.sas.com/ samples/A56936. These data sets are valid for SAS 9 as well as previous versions of SAS. △

The COUNTRIES table contains data that pertains to countries. The Area column contains a country's area in square miles. The UNDate column contains the year a country entered the United Nations, if applicable.

Output 1.3 COUNTRIES (Partial Output)

```
                                  COUNTRIES

 Name                 Capital          Population    Area  Continent         UNDate
 ------------------------------------------------------------------------------------
 Afghanistan          Kabul              17070323  251825  Asia                1946
 Albania              Tirane              3407400   11100  Europe              1955
 Algeria              Algiers            28171132  919595  Africa              1962
 Andorra              Andorra la Vell       64634     200  Europe              1993
 Angola               Luanda              9901050  481300  Africa              1976
 Antigua and Barbuda  St. John's            65644     171  Central America     1981
 Argentina            Buenos Aires       34248705 1073518  South America       1945
 Armenia              Yerevan             3556864   11500  Asia                1992
 Australia            Canberra           18255944 2966200  Australia           1945
 Austria              Vienna              8033746   32400  Europe              1955
 Azerbaijan           Baku                7760064   33400  Asia                1992
 Bahamas              Nassau               275703    5400  Central America     1973
 Bahrain              Manama               591800     300  Asia                1971
 Bangladesh           Dhaka              1.2639E8   57300  Asia                1974
 Barbados             Bridgetown           258534     200  Central America     1966
```

The WORLDCITYCOORDS table contains latitude and longitude data for world cities. Cities in the Western hemisphere have negative longitude coordinates. Cities in the Southern hemisphere have negative latitude coordinates. Coordinates are rounded to the nearest degree.

Output 1.4 WORLDCITYCOORDS (Partial Output)

```
                              WORLDCITCOORDS

            City                Country       Latitude  Longitude
            ------------------------------------------------------
            Kabul               Afghanistan       35        69
            Algiers             Algeria           37         3
            Buenos Aires        Argentina        -34       -59
            Cordoba             Argentina        -31       -64
            Tucuman             Argentina        -27       -65
            Adelaide            Australia        -35       138
            Alice Springs       Australia        -24       134
            Brisbane            Australia        -27       153
            Darwin              Australia        -12       131
            Melbourne           Australia        -38       145
            Perth               Australia        -32       116
            Sydney              Australia        -34       151
            Vienna              Austria           48        16
            Nassau              Bahamas           26       -77
            Chittagong          Bangladesh        22        92
```

The USCITYCOORDS table contains the coordinates for cities in the United States. Because all cities in this table are in the Western hemisphere, all of the longitude coordinates are negative. Coordinates are rounded to the nearest degree.

Output 1.5 USCITYCOORDS (Partial Output)

```
                              USCITYCOORDS

            City              State  Latitude  Longitude
            ---------------------------------------------
            Albany            NY        43        -74
            Albuquerque       NM        36       -106
            Amarillo          TX        35       -102
            Anchorage         AK        61       -150
            Annapolis         MD        39        -77
            Atlanta           GA        34        -84
            Augusta           ME        44        -70
            Austin            TX        30        -98
            Baker             OR        45       -118
            Baltimore         MD        39        -76
            Bangor            ME        45        -69
            Baton Rouge       LA        31        -91
            Birmingham        AL        33        -87
            Bismarck          ND        47       -101
            Boise             ID        43       -116
```

The UNITEDSTATES table contains data that is associated with the states. The Statehood column contains the date when the state was admitted into the Union.

Output 1.6 UNITEDSTATES (Partial Output)

```
                                  UNITEDSTATES

Name                Capital         Population    Area  Continent       Statehood
-----------------------------------------------------------------------------------
Alabama             Montgomery         4227437   52423  North America   14DEC1819
Alaska              Juneau              604929  656400  North America   03JAN1959
Arizona             Phoenix            3974962  114000  North America   14FEB1912
Arkansas            Little Rock        2447996   53200  North America   15JUN1836
California          Sacramento        31518948  163700  North America   09SEP1850
Colorado            Denver             3601298  104100  North America   01AUG1876
Connecticut         Hartford           3309742    5500  North America   09JAN1788
Delaware            Dover               707232    2500  North America   07DEC1787
District of Colum   Washington          612907     100  North America   21FEB1871
Florida             Tallahassee       13814408   65800  North America   03MAR1845
Georgia             Atlanta            6985572   59400  North America   02JAN1788
Hawaii              Honolulu           1183198   10900  Oceania         21AUG1959
Idaho               Boise              1109980   83600  North America   03JUL1890
Illinois            Springfield       11813091   57900  North America   03DEC1818
Indiana             Indianapolis       5769553   36400  North America   11DEC1816
```

The POSTALCODES table contains postal code abbreviations.

Output 1.7 POSTALCODES (Partial Output)

```
                          POSTALCODES

             Name                          Code
             ----------------------------------------
             Alabama                       AL
             Alaska                        AK
             American Samoa                AS
             Arizona                       AZ
             Arkansas                      AR
             California                    CA
             Colorado                      CO
             Connecticut                   CT
             Delaware                      DE
             District Of Columbia          DC
             Florida                       FL
             Georgia                       GA
             Guam                          GU
             Hawaii                        HI
             Idaho                         ID
```

The WORLDTEMPS table contains average high and low temperatures from various international cities.

Output 1.8 WORLDTEMPS (Partial Output)

```
                                 WORLDTEMPS

      City                 Country              AvgHigh      AvgLow
      -------------------------------------------------------------
      Algiers              Algeria                 90          45
      Amsterdam            Netherlands             70          33
      Athens               Greece                  89          41
      Auckland             New Zealand             75          44
      Bangkok              Thailand                95          69
      Beijing              China                   86          17
      Belgrade             Yugoslavia              80          29
      Berlin               Germany                 75          25
      Bogota               Colombia                69          43
      Bombay               India                   90          68
      Bucharest            Romania                 83          24
      Budapest             Hungary                 80          25
      Buenos Aires         Argentina               87          48
      Cairo                Egypt                   95          48
      Calcutta             India                   97          56
```

The OILPROD table contains oil production statistics from oil-producing countries.

Output 1.9 OILPROD (Partial Output)

```
                              OILPROD

                                                Barrels
                    Country                     PerDay
                    --------------------------------------
                    Algeria                   1,400,000
                    Canada                    2,500,000
                    China                     3,000,000
                    Egypt                       900,000
                    Indonesia                 1,500,000
                    Iran                      4,000,000
                    Iraq                        600,000
                    Kuwait                    2,500,000
                    Libya                     1,500,000
                    Mexico                    3,400,000
                    Nigeria                   2,000,000
                    Norway                    3,500,000
                    Oman                        900,000
                    Saudi Arabia              9,000,000
                    United States of America  8,000,000
```

The OILRSRVS table lists approximate oil reserves of oil-producing countries.

Output 1.10 OILRSRVS (Partial Output)

```
                                  OILRSRVS

              Country                              Barrels
              ---------------------------------------------------
              Algeria                         9,200,000,000
              Canada                          7,000,000,000
              China                          25,000,000,000
              Egypt                           4,000,000,000
              Gabon                           1,000,000,000
              Indonesia                       5,000,000,000
              Iran                           90,000,000,000
              Iraq                          110,000,000,000
              Kuwait                         95,000,000,000
              Libya                          30,000,000,000
              Mexico                         50,000,000,000
              Nigeria                        16,000,000,000
              Norway                         11,000,000,000
              Saudi Arabia                  260,000,000,000
              United Arab Emirates             100,000,000
```

The CONTINENTS table contains geographic data that relates to world continents.

Output 1.11 CONTINENTS

```
                                  CONTINENTS

Name                Area  HighPoint          Height  LowPoint           Depth
-----------------------------------------------------------------------------
Africa           11506000 Kilimanjaro         19340  Lake Assal          -512
Antarctica        5500000 Vinson Massif       16860                         .
Asia             16988000 Everest             29028  Dead Sea           -1302
Australia         2968000 Kosciusko            7310  Lake Eyre            -52
Central America         .                          .                        .
Europe            3745000 El'brus             18510  Caspian Sea          -92
North America     9390000 McKinley            20320  Death Valley        -282
Oceania                 .                          .                        .
South America     6795000 Aconcagua           22834  Valdes Peninsul     -131
```

The FEATURES table contains statistics that describe various types of geographical features, such as oceans, lakes, and mountains.

Output 1.12 FEATURES (Partial Output)

```
                                    FEATURES

 Name            Type         Location         Area    Height     Depth    Length

 Aconcagua       Mountain     Argentina           .     22834         .         .
 Amazon          River        South America       .         .         .      4000
 Amur            River        Asia                .         .         .      2700
 Andaman         Sea                          218100         .      3667         .
 Angel Falls     Waterfall    Venezuela           .      3212         .         .
 Annapurna       Mountain     Nepal               .     26504         .         .
 Aral Sea        Lake         Asia            25300         .       222         .
 Ararat          Mountain     Turkey              .     16804         .         .
 Arctic          Ocean                       5105700         .     17880         .
 Atlantic        Ocean                      33420000         .     28374         .
 Baffin          Island       Arctic         183810         .         .         .
 Baltic          Sea                         146500         .       180         .
 Baykal          Lake         Russia          11780         .      5315         .
 Bering          Sea                         873000         .      4893         .
 Black           Sea                         196100         .      3906         .
```

CHAPTER

2

Retrieving Data from a Single Table

Overview of the SELECT Statement   **12**
    SELECT and FROM Clauses   **12**
    WHERE Clause   **13**
    ORDER BY Clause   **13**
    GROUP BY Clause   **13**
    HAVING Clause   **13**
    Ordering the SELECT Statement   **14**
Selecting Columns in a Table   **14**
    Selecting All Columns in a Table   **14**
    Selecting Specific Columns in a Table   **15**
    Eliminating Duplicate Rows from the Query Results   **16**
    Determining the Structure of a Table   **17**
Creating New Columns   **18**
    Adding Text to Output   **18**
    Calculating Values   **19**
    Assigning a Column Alias   **20**
    Referring to a Calculated Column by Alias   **21**
    Assigning Values Conditionally   **21**
        Using a Simple CASE Expression   **22**
        Using the CASE-OPERAND Form   **23**
    Replacing Missing Values   **24**
    Specifying Column Attributes   **24**
Sorting Data   **25**
    Sorting by Column   **26**
    Sorting by Multiple Columns   **26**
    Specifying a Sort Order   **27**
    Sorting by Calculated Column   **28**
    Sorting by Column Position   **29**
    Sorting by Columns That Are Not Selected   **29**
    Specifying a Different Sorting Sequence   **30**
    Sorting Columns That Contain Missing Values   **30**
Retrieving Rows That Satisfy a Condition   **31**
    Using a Simple WHERE Clause   **31**
    Retrieving Rows Based on a Comparison   **32**
    Retrieving Rows That Satisfy Multiple Conditions   **33**
    Using Other Conditional Operators   **34**
        Using the IN Operator   **35**
        Using the IS MISSING Operator   **36**
        Using the BETWEEN-AND Operators   **36**
        Using the LIKE Operator   **37**
    Using Truncated String Comparison Operators   **38**

Using a WHERE Clause with Missing Values   **38**
Summarizing Data   **40**
   Using Aggregate Functions   **40**
   Summarizing Data with a WHERE Clause   **41**
     Using the MEAN Function with a WHERE Clause   **41**
   Displaying Sums   **42**
   Combining Data from Multiple Rows into a Single Row   **42**
   Remerging Summary Statistics   **42**
   Using Aggregate Functions with Unique Values   **44**
     Counting Unique Values   **44**
     Counting Nonmissing Values   **45**
     Counting All Rows   **45**
   Summarizing Data with Missing Values   **45**
     Finding Errors Caused by Missing Values   **46**
Grouping Data   **47**
   Grouping by One Column   **47**
   Grouping without Summarizing   **47**
   Grouping by Multiple Columns   **48**
   Grouping and Sorting Data   **49**
   Grouping with Missing Values   **50**
     Finding Grouping Errors Caused by Missing Values   **50**
Filtering Grouped Data   **51**
   Using a Simple HAVING Clause   **51**
   Choosing between HAVING and WHERE   **52**
   Using HAVING with Aggregate Functions   **53**
Validating a Query   **53**

Overview of the SELECT Statement

This chapter shows you how to

- retrieve data from a single table by using the SELECT statement
- validate the correctness of a SELECT statement by using the VALIDATE statement.

With the SELECT statement, you can retrieve data from tables or data that is described by SAS data views.

Note: The examples in this chapter retrieve data from tables that are SAS data sets. However, you can use all of the operations that are described here with SAS data views. △

The SELECT statement is the primary tool of PROC SQL. You use it to identify, retrieve, and manipulate columns of data from a table. You can also use several optional clauses within the SELECT statement to place restrictions on a query.

SELECT and FROM Clauses

The following simple SELECT statement is sufficient to produce a useful result:

```
select Name
   from sql.countries;
```

The SELECT statement must contain a SELECT clause and a FROM clause, both of which are required in a PROC SQL query. This SELECT statement contains

□ a SELECT clause that lists the Name column

□ a FROM clause that lists the table in which the Name column resides.

WHERE Clause

The WHERE clause enables you to restrict the data that you retrieve by specifying a condition that each row of the table must satisfy. PROC SQL output includes only those rows that satisfy the condition. The following SELECT statement contains a WHERE clause that restricts the query output to only those countries that have a population that is greater than 5,000,000 people:

```
select Name
   from sql.countries
   where Population gt 5000000;
```

ORDER BY Clause

The ORDER BY clause enables you to sort the output from a table by one or more columns; that is, you can put character values in either ascending or descending alphabetical order, and you can put numerical values in either ascending or descending numerical order. The default order is ascending. For example, you can modify the previous example to list the data by descending population:

```
select Name
   from sql.countries
   where Population gt 5000000
   order by Population desc;
```

GROUP BY Clause

The GROUP BY clause enables you to break query results into subsets of rows. When you use the GROUP BY clause, you use an aggregate function in the SELECT clause or a HAVING clause to instruct PROC SQL how to group the data. For details about aggregate functions, see "Summarizing Data" on page 40. PROC SQL calculates the aggregate function separately for each group. When you do not use an aggregate function, PROC SQL treats the GROUP BY clause as if it were an ORDER BY clause, and any aggregate functions are applied to the entire table.

The following query uses the SUM function to list the total population of each continent. The GROUP BY clause groups the countries by continent, and the ORDER BY clause puts the continents in alphabetical order:

```
select Continent, sum(Population)
   from sql.countries
   group by Continent
   order by Continent;
```

HAVING Clause

The HAVING clause works with the GROUP BY clause to restrict the groups in a query's results based on a given condition. PROC SQL applies the HAVING condition after grouping the data and applying aggregate functions. For example, the following query restricts the groups to include only the continents of Asia and Europe:

```
select Continent, sum(Population)
   from sql.countries
   group by Continent
   having Continent in ('Asia', 'Europe')
   order by Continent;
```

Ordering the SELECT Statement

When you construct a SELECT statement, you must specify the clauses in the following order:

1 SELECT

2 FROM

3 WHERE

4 GROUP BY

5 HAVING

6 ORDER BY

Note: Only the SELECT and FROM clauses are required. △

The PROC SQL SELECT statement and its clauses are discussed in further detail in the following sections.

Selecting Columns in a Table

When you retrieve data from a table, you can select one or more columns by using variations of the basic SELECT statement.

Selecting All Columns in a Table

Use an asterisk in the SELECT clause to select all columns in a table. The following example selects all columns in the SQL.USCITYCOORDS table, which contains latitude and longitude values for U.S. cities:

```
proc sql outobs=12;
   title 'U.S. Cities with Their States and Coordinates';
   select *
      from sql.uscitycoords;
```

Note: The OUTOBS= option limits the number of rows (observations) in the output. OUTOBS= is similar to the OBS= data set option. OUTOBS= is used throughout this document to limit the number of rows that are displayed in examples. △

Note: In the tables used in these examples, latitude values that are south of the Equator are negative. Longitude values that are west of the Prime Meridian are also negative. △

Output 2.1 Selecting All Columns in a Table

```
         U.S. Cities with Their States and Coordinates

         City                 State  Latitude  Longitude
         ------------------------------------------------
         Albany               NY        43        -74
         Albuquerque          NM        36       -106
         Amarillo             TX        35       -102
         Anchorage            AK        61       -150
         Annapolis            MD        39        -77
         Atlanta              GA        34        -84
         Augusta              ME        44        -70
         Austin               TX        30        -98
         Baker                OR        45       -118
         Baltimore            MD        39        -76
         Bangor               ME        45        -69
         Baton Rouge          LA        31        -91
```

Note: When you select all columns, PROC SQL displays the columns in the order in which they are stored in the table. △

Selecting Specific Columns in a Table

To select a specific column in a table, list the name of the column in the SELECT clause. The following example selects only the City column in the SQL.USCITYCOORDS table:

```
proc sql outobs=12;
   title 'Names of U.S. Cities';
   select City
      from sql.uscitycoords;
```

Output 2.2 Selecting One Column

```
                    Names of U.S. Cities

                    City
                    -------------------
                    Albany
                    Albuquerque
                    Amarillo
                    Anchorage
                    Annapolis
                    Atlanta
                    Augusta
                    Austin
                    Baker
                    Baltimore
                    Bangor
                    Baton Rouge
```

If you want to select more than one column, then you must separate the names of the columns with commas, as in this example, which selects the City and State columns in the SQL.USCITYCOORDS table:

```
proc sql outobs=12;
    title 'U.S. Cities and Their States';
    select City, State
        from sql.uscitycoords;
```

Output 2.3   Selecting Multiple Columns

```
                        U.S. Cities and Their States

                      City                    State
                      ------------------------------
                      Albany                  NY
                      Albuquerque             NM
                      Amarillo                TX
                      Anchorage               AK
                      Annapolis               MD
                      Atlanta                 GA
                      Augusta                 ME
                      Austin                  TX
                      Baker                   OR
                      Baltimore               MD
                      Bangor                  ME
                      Baton Rouge             LA
```

Note: When you select specific columns, PROC SQL displays the columns in the order in which you specify them in the SELECT clause. △

Eliminating Duplicate Rows from the Query Results

In some cases, you might want to find only the unique values in a column. For example, if you want to find the unique continents in which U.S. states are located, then you might begin by constructing the following query:

```
proc sql outobs=12;
    title 'Continents of the United States';
    select Continent
        from sql.unitedstates;
```

Output 2.4 Selecting a Column with Duplicate Values

```
                        Continents of the United States

             Continent
             ----------------------------------
             North America
             North America
             North America
             North America
             North America
             North America
             North America
             North America
             North America
             North America
             North America
             Oceania
```

You can eliminate the duplicate rows from the results by using the DISTINCT keyword in the SELECT clause. Compare the previous example with the following query, which uses the DISTINCT keyword to produce a single row of output for each continent that is in the SQL.UNITEDSTATES table:

```
proc sql;
   title 'Continents of the United States';
   select distinct Continent
      from sql.unitedstates;
```

Output 2.5 Eliminating Duplicate Values

```
                        Continents of the United States

             Continent
             ----------------------------------
             North America
             Oceania
```

Note: When you specify all of a table's columns in a SELECT clause with the DISTINCT keyword, PROC SQL eliminates duplicate rows, or rows in which the values in all of the columns match, from the results. △

Determining the Structure of a Table

To obtain a list of all of the columns in a table and their attributes, you can use the DESCRIBE TABLE statement. The following example generates a description of the SQL.UNITEDSTATES table. PROC SQL writes the description to the log.

```
proc sql;
   describe table sql.unitedstates;
```

Output 2.6   Determining the Structure of a Table (Partial Log)

```
NOTE: SQL table SQL.UNITEDSTATES was created like:

create table SQL.UNITEDSTATES( bufsize=12288 )
  (
   Name char(35) format=$35. informat=$35. label='Name',
   Capital char(35) format=$35. informat=$35. label='Capital',
   Population num format=BEST8. informat=BEST8. label='Population',
   Area num format=BEST8. informat=BEST8.,
   Continent char(35) format=$35. informat=$35. label='Continent',
   Statehood num
  );
```

Creating New Columns

In addition to selecting columns that are stored in a table, you can create new columns that exist for the duration of the query. These columns can contain text or calculations. PROC SQL writes the columns that you create as if they were columns from the table.

Adding Text to Output

You can add text to the output by including a string expression, or literal expression, in a query. The following query includes two strings as additional columns in the output:

```
proc sql outobs=12;
   title 'U.S. Postal Codes';
   select 'Postal code for', Name, 'is', Code
      from sql.postalcodes;
```

Output 2.7   Adding Text to Output

```
                         U.S. Postal Codes

                     Name                                   Code
           -----------------------------------------------------
           Postal code for  Alabama                   is  AL
           Postal code for  Alaska                    is  AK
           Postal code for  American Samoa            is  AS
           Postal code for  Arizona                   is  AZ
           Postal code for  Arkansas                  is  AR
           Postal code for  California                is  CA
           Postal code for  Colorado                  is  CO
           Postal code for  Connecticut               is  CT
           Postal code for  Delaware                  is  DE
           Postal code for  District Of Columbia      is  DC
           Postal code for  Florida                   is  FL
           Postal code for  Georgia                   is  GA
```

To prevent the column headings Name and Code from printing, you can assign a label that starts with a special character to each of the columns. PROC SQL does not output the column name when a label is assigned, and it does not output labels that begin with special characters. For example, you could use the following query to suppress the column headings that PROC SQL displayed in the previous example:

```
proc sql outobs=12;
   title 'U.S. Postal Codes';
   select 'Postal code for', Name label='#', 'is', Code label='#'
      from sql.postalcodes;
```

Output 2.8 Suppressing Column Headings in Output

```
                          U.S. Postal Codes


         ---------------------------------------------------------
         Postal code for  Alabama                       is  AL
         Postal code for  Alaska                        is  AK
         Postal code for  American Samoa                is  AS
         Postal code for  Arizona                       is  AZ
         Postal code for  Arkansas                      is  AR
         Postal code for  California                    is  CA
         Postal code for  Colorado                      is  CO
         Postal code for  Connecticut                   is  CT
         Postal code for  Delaware                      is  DE
         Postal code for  District Of Columbia          is  DC
         Postal code for  Florida                       is  FL
         Postal code for  Georgia                       is  GA
```

Calculating Values

You can perform calculations with values that you retrieve from numeric columns. The following example converts temperatures in the SQL.WORLDTEMPS table from Fahrenheit to Celsius:

```
proc sql outobs=12;
   title 'Low Temperatures in Celsius';
   select City, (AvgLow - 32) * 5/9 format=4.1
      from sql.worldtemps;
```

Note: This example uses the FORMAT attribute to modify the format of the calculated output. See "Specifying Column Attributes" on page 24 for more information. △

Output 2.9   Calculating Values

```
                    Low Temperatures in Celsius

                  City
                  -------------------------
                  Algiers                7.2
                  Amsterdam              0.6
                  Athens                 5.0
                  Auckland               6.7
                  Bangkok               20.6
                  Beijing               -8.3
                  Belgrade              -1.7
                  Berlin                -3.9
                  Bogota                 6.1
                  Bombay                20.0
                  Bucharest             -4.4
                  Budapest              -3.9
```

Assigning a Column Alias

By specifying a column alias, you can assign a new name to any column within a
PROC SQL query. The new name must follow the rules for SAS names. The name
persists only for that query.

When you use an alias to name a column, you can use the alias to reference the
column later in the query. PROC SQL uses the alias as the column heading in output.
The following example assigns an alias of LowCelsius to the calculated column from the
previous example:

```
proc sql outobs=12;
    title 'Low Temperatures in Celsius';
    select City, (AvgLow - 32) * 5/9 as LowCelsius format=4.1
        from sql.worldtemps;
```

Output 2.10   Assigning a Column Alias to a Calculated Column

```
                    Low Temperatures in Celsius

              City                 LowCelsius
              ---------------------------------
              Algiers                     7.2
              Amsterdam                   0.6
              Athens                      5.0
              Auckland                    6.7
              Bangkok                    20.6
              Beijing                    -8.3
              Belgrade                   -1.7
              Berlin                     -3.9
              Bogota                      6.1
              Bombay                     20.0
              Bucharest                  -4.4
              Budapest                   -3.9
```

Referring to a Calculated Column by Alias

When you use a column alias to refer to a calculated value, you must use the CALCULATED keyword with the alias to inform PROC SQL that the value is calculated within the query. The following example uses two calculated values, LowC and HighC, to calculate a third value, Range:

```
proc sql outobs=12;
   title 'Range of High and Low Temperatures in Celsius';
      select City, (AvgHigh - 32) * 5/9 as HighC format=5.1,
                   (AvgLow - 32) * 5/9 as LowC format=5.1,
                   (calculated HighC - calculated LowC)
                    as Range format=4.1
   from sql.worldtemps;
```

Note: You can specify a calculated column only in a SELECT clause or a WHERE clause. △

Output 2.11   Referring to a Calculated Column by Alias

```
            Range of High and Low Temperatures in Celsius

            City              HighC   LowC   Range
            -------------------------------------------
            Algiers            32.2    7.2   25.0
            Amsterdam          21.1    0.6   20.6
            Athens             31.7    5.0   26.7
            Auckland           23.9    6.7   17.2
            Bangkok            35.0   20.6   14.4
            Beijing            30.0   -8.3   38.3
            Belgrade           26.7   -1.7   28.3
            Berlin             23.9   -3.9   27.8
            Bogota             20.6    6.1   14.4
            Bombay             32.2   20.0   12.2
            Bucharest          28.3   -4.4   32.8
            Budapest           26.7   -3.9   30.6
```

Note: Because this query sets a numeric format of 4.1 on the HighC, LowC, and Range columns, the values in those columns are rounded to the nearest tenth. As a result of the rounding, some of the values in the HighC and LowC columns do not reflect the range value output for the Range column. When you round numeric data values, this type of error sometimes occurs. If you want to avoid this problem, then you can specify additional decimal places in the format. △

Assigning Values Conditionally

CASE expressions enable you to interpret and change some or all of the data values in a column to make the data more useful or meaningful.

Using a Simple CASE Expression

You can use conditional logic within a query by using a CASE expression to conditionally assign a value. You can use a CASE expression anywhere that you can use a column name.

The following table, which is used in the next example, describes the world climate zones (rounded to the nearest degree) that exist between Location 1 and Location 2:

Table 2.1 World Climate Zones

Climate zone	Location 1	Latitude at Location 1	Location 2	Latitude at Location 2
North Frigid	North Pole	90	Arctic Circle	67
North Temperate	Arctic Circle	67	Tropic of Cancer	23
Torrid	Tropic of Cancer	23	Tropic of Capricorn	-23
South Temperate	Tropic of Capricorn	-23	Antarctic Circle	-67
South Frigid	Antarctic Circle	-67	South Pole	-90

In this example, a CASE expression determines the climate zone for each city based on the value in the Latitude column in the SQL.WORLDCITYCOORDS table. The query also assigns an alias of ClimateZone to the value. You must close the CASE logic with the END keyword.

```
proc sql outobs=12;
    title 'Climate Zones of World Cities';
    select City, Country, Latitude,
          case
              when Latitude gt 67 then 'North Frigid'
              when 67 ge Latitude ge 23 then 'North Temperate'
              when 23 gt Latitude gt -23 then 'Torrid'
              when -23 ge Latitude ge -67 then 'South Temperate'
              else 'South Frigid'
          end as ClimateZone
    from sql.worldcitycoords
    order by City;
```

Output 2.12 Using a Simple CASE Expression

```
                        Climate Zones of World Cities

      City                        Country              Latitude  ClimateZone
      ------------------------------------------------------------------------
      Abadan                      Iran                       30  North Temperate
      Acapulco                    Mexico                     17  Torrid
      Accra                       Ghana                       5  Torrid
      Adana                       Turkey                     37  North Temperate
      Addis Ababa                 Ethiopia                    9  Torrid
      Adelaide                    Australia                 -35  South Temperate
      Aden                        Yemen                      13  Torrid
      Ahmenabad                   India                      22  Torrid
      Algiers                     Algeria                    37  North Temperate
      Alice Springs               Australia                 -24  South Temperate
      Amman                       Jordan                     32  North Temperate
      Amsterdam                   Netherlands                52  North Temperate
```

Using the CASE-OPERAND Form

You can also construct a CASE expression by using the CASE-OPERAND form, as in the following example. This example selects states and assigns them to a region based on the value of the Continent column:

```
proc sql outobs=12;
   title 'Assigning Regions to Continents';
   select Name, Continent,
        case Continent
            when 'North America' then 'Continental U.S.'
            when 'Oceania' then 'Pacific Islands'
            else 'None'
        end as Region
     from sql.unitedstates;
```

Note: When you use the CASE-OPERAND form of the CASE expression, the conditions must all be equality tests; that is, they cannot use comparison operators or other types of operators, as are used in "Using a Simple CASE Expression" on page 22. △

Output 2.13 Using a CASE Expression in the CASE-OPERAND Form

```
                      Assigning Regions to Continents

   Name                       Continent              Region
   -----------------------------------------------------------------------
   Alabama                    North America          Continental U.S.
   Alaska                     North America          Continental U.S.
   Arizona                    North America          Continental U.S.
   Arkansas                   North America          Continental U.S.
   California                 North America          Continental U.S.
   Colorado                   North America          Continental U.S.
   Connecticut                North America          Continental U.S.
   Delaware                   North America          Continental U.S.
   District of Columbia       North America          Continental U.S.
   Florida                    North America          Continental U.S.
   Georgia                    North America          Continental U.S.
   Hawaii                     Oceania                Pacific Islands
```

Replacing Missing Values

The COALESCE function enables you to replace missing values in a column with a new value that you specify. For every row that the query processes, the COALESCE function checks each of its arguments until it finds a nonmissing value, then returns that value. If all of the arguments are missing values, then the COALESCE function returns a missing value. For example, the following query replaces missing values in the LowPoint column in the SQL.CONTINENTS table with the words **Not Available**:

```
proc sql;
   title 'Continental Low Points';
   select Name, coalesce(LowPoint, 'Not Available') as LowPoint
      from sql.continents;
```

Output 2.14   Using the COALESCE Function to Replace Missing Values

```
                          Continental Low Points

        Name                           LowPoint
        ----------------------------------------------------------------
        Africa                         Lake Assal
        Antarctica                     Not Available
        Asia                           Dead Sea
        Australia                      Lake Eyre
        Central America and Caribbean  Not Available
        Europe                         Caspian Sea
        North America                  Death Valley
        Oceania                        Not Available
        South America                  Valdes Peninsula
```

The following CASE expression shows another way to perform the same replacement of missing values; however, the COALESCE function requires fewer lines of code to obtain the same results:

```
proc sql;
   title 'Continental Low Points';
   select Name, case
                   when LowPoint is missing then 'Not Available'
                   else Lowpoint
                end as LowPoint
      from sql.continents;
```

Specifying Column Attributes

You can specify the following column attributes, which determine how SAS data is displayed:
- □ FORMAT=
- □ INFORMAT=
- □ LABEL=
- □ LENGTH=

If you do not specify these attributes, then PROC SQL uses attributes that are already saved in the table or, if no attributes are saved, then it uses the default attributes.

The following example assigns a label of **state** to the Name column and a format of COMMA10. to the Area column:

```
proc sql outobs=12;
   title 'Areas of U.S. States in Square Miles';
   select Name label='State', Area format=comma10.
      from sql.unitedstates;
```

Note: Using the LABEL= keyword is optional. For example, the following two select clauses are the same:

```
select Name label='State', Area format=comma10.
```

```
select Name 'State', Area format=comma10.
```

△

Output 2.15 Specifying Column Attributes

```
            Areas of U.S. States in Square Miles

         State                                    Area
         ------------------------------------------------
         Alabama                                52,423
         Alaska                                656,400
         Arizona                               114,000
         Arkansas                               53,200
         California                            163,700
         Colorado                              104,100
         Connecticut                             5,500
         Delaware                                2,500
         District of Columbia                      100
         Florida                                65,800
         Georgia                                59,400
         Hawaii                                 10,900
```

Sorting Data

You can sort query results with an ORDER BY clause by specifying any of the columns in the table, including columns that are not selected or columns that are calculated.

Unless an ORDER BY clause is included in the SELECT statement, then a particular order to the output rows, such as the order in which the rows are encountered in the queried table, cannot be guaranteed, even if an index is present. Without an ORDER BY clause, the order of the output rows is determined by the internal processing of PROC SQL, the default collating sequence of SAS, and your operating environment. Therefore, if you want your result table to appear in a particular order, then use the ORDER BY clause.

For more information and examples see the ORDER BY clause in *Base SAS Procedures Guide*.

Sorting by Column

The following example selects countries and their populations from the
SQL.COUNTRIES table and orders the results by population:

```
proc sql outobs=12;
   title 'Country Populations';
   select Name, Population format=comma10.
      from sql.countries
      order by Population;
```

Note: When you use an ORDER BY clause, you change the order of the output but
not the order of the rows that are stored in the table. △

Note: The PROC SQL default sort order is ascending. △

Output 2.16   Sorting by Column

```
                            Country Populations

               Name                              Population
               ------------------------------------------------
               Vatican City                           1,010
               Tuvalu                                10,099
               Nauru                                 10,099
               Turks and Caicos Islands              12,119
               Leeward Islands                       12,119
               Cayman Islands                        23,228
               San Marino                            24,238
               Liechtenstein                         30,297
               Gibraltar                             30,297
               Monaco                                31,307
               Saint Kitts and Nevis                 41,406
               Marshall Islands                      54,535
```

Sorting by Multiple Columns

You can sort by more than one column by specifying the column names, separated by
commas, in the ORDER BY clause. The following example sorts the SQL.COUNTRIES
table by two columns, Continent and Name:

```
proc sql outobs=12;
   title 'Countries, Sorted by Continent and Name';
   select Name, Continent
      from sql.countries
      order by Continent, Name;
```

Output 2.17   Sorting by Multiple Columns

```
                 Countries, Sorted by Continent and Name

        Name                                 Continent
        ---------------------------------------------------------------------
        Bermuda
        Iceland
        Kalaallit Nunaat
        Algeria                              Africa
        Angola                               Africa
        Benin                                Africa
        Botswana                             Africa
        Burkina Faso                         Africa
        Burundi                              Africa
        Cameroon                             Africa
        Cape Verde                           Africa
        Central African  Republic            Africa
```

Note: The results list countries without continents first because PROC SQL sorts missing values first in an ascending sort. △

Specifying a Sort Order

To order the results, specify ASC for ascending or DESC for descending. You can specify a sort order for each column in the ORDER BY clause.

When you specify multiple columns in the ORDER BY clause, the first column determines the primary row order of the results. Subsequent columns determine the order of rows that have the same value for the primary sort. The following example sorts the SQL.FEATURES table by feature type and name:

```
proc sql outobs=12;
   title 'World Topographical Features';
   select Name, Type
      from sql.features
      order by Type desc, Name;
```

Note: The ASC keyword is optional because the PROC SQL default sort order is ascending. △

Output 2.18   Specifying a Sort Order

```
                         World Topographical Features

                   Name               Type
                   ----------------------------
                   Angel Falls        Waterfall
                   Niagara Falls      Waterfall
                   Tugela Falls       Waterfall
                   Yosemite           Waterfall
                   Andaman            Sea
                   Baltic             Sea
                   Bering             Sea
                   Black              Sea
                   Caribbean          Sea
                   Gulf of Mexico     Sea
                   Hudson Bay         Sea
                   Mediterranean      Sea
```

Sorting by Calculated Column

You can sort by a calculated column by specifying its alias in the ORDER BY clause. The following example calculates population densities and then performs a sort on the calculated Density column:

```
proc sql outobs=12;
    title 'World Population Densities per Square Mile';
    select Name, Population format=comma12., Area format=comma8.,
          Population/Area as Density format=comma10.
       from sql.countries
       order by Density desc;
```

Output 2.19   Sorting by Calculated Column

```
                   World Population Densities per Square Mile

         Name                          Population      Area      Density
         ----------------------------------------------------------------
         Hong Kong                      5,857,414        400       14,644
         Singapore                      2,887,301        200       14,437
         Luxembourg                       405,980        100        4,060
         Malta                            370,633        100        3,706
         Maldives                         254,495        100        2,545
         Bangladesh                   126,387,850     57,300        2,206
         Bahrain                          591,800        300        1,973
         Taiwan                        21,509,839     14,000        1,536
         Channel Islands                  146,436        100        1,464
         Barbados                         258,534        200        1,293
         Korea, South                  45,529,277     38,300        1,189
         Mauritius                      1,128,057      1,000        1,128
```

Sorting by Column Position

You can sort by any column within the SELECT clause by specifying its numerical position. By specifying a position instead of a name, you can sort by a calculated column that has no alias. The following example does not assign an alias to the calculated density column. Instead, the column position of 4 in the ORDER BY clause refers to the position of the calculated column in the SELECT clause:

```
proc sql outobs=12;
    title 'World Population Densities per Square Mile';
    select Name, Population format=comma12., Area format=comma8.,
        Population/Area format=comma10. label='Density'
      from sql.countries
      order by 4 desc;
```

Note: PROC SQL uses a label, if one has been assigned, as a heading for a column that does not have an alias. △

Output 2.20 Sorting by Column Position

```
                   World Population Densities per Square Mile

   Name                                 Population      Area     Density
   -----------------------------------------------------------------------
   Hong Kong                             5,857,414       400      14,644
   Singapore                             2,887,301       200      14,437
   Luxembourg                              405,980       100       4,060
   Malta                                   370,633       100       3,706
   Maldives                                254,495       100       2,545
   Bangladesh                          126,387,850    57,300       2,206
   Bahrain                                 591,800       300       1,973
   Taiwan                               21,509,839    14,000       1,536
   Channel Islands                         146,436       100       1,464
   Barbados                                258,534       200       1,293
   Korea, South                         45,529,277    38,300       1,189
   Mauritius                             1,128,057     1,000       1,128
```

Sorting by Columns That Are Not Selected

You can sort query results by columns that are not included in the query. For example, the following query returns all the rows in the SQL.COUNTRIES table and sorts them by population, even though the Population column is not included in the query:

```
proc sql outobs=12;
    title 'Countries, Sorted by Population';
    select Name, Continent
      from sql.countries
      order by Population;
```

Output 2.21 Sorting by Columns That are not Selected

```
                         Countries, Sorted by Population

        Name                               Continent
        ------------------------------------------------------------------
        Vatican City                       Europe
        Tuvalu                             Oceania
        Nauru                              Oceania
        Turks and Caicos Islands           Central America and Caribbean
        Leeward Islands                    Central America and Caribbean
        Cayman Islands                     Central America and Caribbean
        San Marino                         Europe
        Liechtenstein                      Europe
        Gibraltar                          Europe
        Monaco                             Europe
        Saint Kitts and Nevis              Central America and Caribbean
        Marshall Islands                   Oceania
```

Specifying a Different Sorting Sequence

SORTSEQ= is a PROC SQL statement option that specifies the sorting sequence for PROC SQL to use when a query contains an ORDER BY clause. Use this option only if you want to use a sorting sequence other than your operating environment's default sorting sequence. Possible values include ASCII, EBCDIC, and some languages other than English. For example, in an operating environment that supports the EBCDIC sorting sequence, you could use the following option in the PROC SQL statement to set the sorting sequence to EBCDIC:

```
proc sql sortseq=ebcdic;
```

Note: SORTSEQ= affects only the ORDER BY clause. It does not override your operating environment's default comparison operations for the WHERE clause. △

Operating Environment Information: See the SAS documentation for your operating environment for more information about the default and other sorting sequences for your operating environment. △

Sorting Columns That Contain Missing Values

PROC SQL sorts nulls, or missing values, before character or numeric data; therefore, when you specify ascending order, missing values appear first in the query results.

The following example sorts the rows in the CONTINENTS table by the LowPoint column:

```
proc sql;
    title 'Continents, Sorted by Low Point';
    select Name, LowPoint
       from sql.continents
       order by LowPoint;
```

Because three continents have a missing value in the LowPoint column, those continents appear first in the output. Note that because the query does not specify a secondary sort, rows that have the same value in the LowPoint column, such as the first three rows of output, are not displayed in any particular order. In general, if you do not explicitly specify a sort order, then PROC SQL output is not guaranteed to be in any particular order.

Output 2.22 Sorting Columns That Contain Missing Values

```
                        Continents, Sorted by Low Point

         Name                             LowPoint
         ----------------------------------------------------------------------
         Central America and Caribbean
         Antarctica
         Oceania
         Europe                           Caspian Sea
         Asia                             Dead Sea
         North America                    Death Valley
         Africa                           Lake Assal
         Australia                        Lake Eyre
         South America                    Valdes Peninsula
```

Retrieving Rows That Satisfy a Condition

The WHERE clause enables you to retrieve only rows from a table that satisfy a condition. WHERE clauses can contain any of the columns in a table, including columns that are not selected.

Using a Simple WHERE Clause

The following example uses a WHERE clause to find all countries that are in the continent of Europe and their populations:

```
proc sql outobs=12;
   title 'Countries in Europe';
   select Name, Population format=comma10.
      from sql.countries
      where Continent = 'Europe';
```

Output 2.23   Using a Simple WHERE Clause

```
                          Countries in Europe

          Name                              Population
          -------------------------------------------------
          Albania                             3,407,400
          Andorra                                64,634
          Austria                             8,033,746
          Belarus                            10,508,000
          Belgium                            10,162,614
          Bosnia and Herzegovina              4,697,040
          Bulgaria                            8,887,111
          Channel Islands                       146,436
          Croatia                             4,744,505
          Czech Republic                     10,511,029
          Denmark                             5,239,356
          England                            49,293,170
```

Retrieving Rows Based on a Comparison

You can use comparison operators in a WHERE clause to select different subsets of data. The following table lists the comparison operators that you can use:

Table 2.2   Comparison Operators

Symbol	Mnemonic Equivalent	Definition	Example
=	EQ	equal to	where Name = 'Asia';
^= or ~= or ¬= or <>	NE	not equal to	where Name ne 'Africa';
>	GT	greater than	where Area > 10000;
<	LT	less than	where Depth < 5000;
>=	GE	greater than or equal to	where Statehood >= '01jan1860'd;
<=	LE	less than or equal to	where Population <= 5000000;

The following example subsets the SQL.UNITEDSTATES table by including only states with populations greater than 5,000,000 people:

```
proc sql;
   title 'States with Populations over 5,000,000';
   select Name, Population format=comma10.
      from sql.unitedstates
      where Population gt 5000000
      order by Population desc;
```

Output 2.24 Retrieving Rows Based on a Comparison

```
                    States with Populations over 5,000,000

        Name                                       Population
        ------------------------------------------------------
        California                                 31,518,948
        New York                                   18,377,334
        Texas                                      18,209,994
        Florida                                    13,814,408
        Pennsylvania                               12,167,566
        Illinois                                   11,813,091
        Ohio                                       11,200,790
        Michigan                                    9,571,318
        New Jersey                                  7,957,196
        North Carolina                             7,013,950
        Georgia                                     6,985,572
        Virginia                                    6,554,851
        Massachusetts                              6,071,816
        Indiana                                    5,769,553
        Washington                                 5,307,322
        Missouri                                   5,285,610
        Tennessee                                  5,149,273
        Wisconsin                                  5,087,770
        Maryland                                   5,014,048
```

Retrieving Rows That Satisfy Multiple Conditions

You can use logical, or Boolean, operators to construct a WHERE clause that contains two or more expressions. The following table lists the logical operators that you can use:

Table 2.3 Logical (Boolean) Operators

Symbol	Mnemonic Equivalent	Definition	Example
&	AND	specifies that both the previous and following conditions must be true	`Continent = 'Asia' and Population > 5000000`
! or | or ¦	OR	specifies that either the previous or the following condition must be true	`Population < 1000000 or Population > 5000000`
^ or ~ or ¬	NOT	specifies that the following condition must be false	`Continent not 'Africa'`

The following example uses two expressions to include only countries that are in Africa and that have a population greater than 20,000,000 people:

```
proc sql;
   title 'Countries in Africa with Populations over 20,000,000';
   select Name, Population format=comma10.
      from sql.countries
      where Continent = 'Africa' and Population gt 20000000
      order by Population desc;
```

Output 2.25 Retrieving Rows That Satisfy Multiple Conditions

```
              Countries in Africa with Populations over 20,000,000

              Name                             Population
              -----------------------------------------------------
              Nigeria                           99,062,003
              Egypt                             59,912,259
              Ethiopia                          59,291,170
              South Africa                      44,365,873
              Congo, Democratic Republic of     43,106,529
              Sudan                             29,711,229
              Morocco                           28,841,705
              Kenya                             28,520,558
              Tanzania                          28,263,033
              Algeria                           28,171,132
              Uganda                            20,055,584
```

Note: You can use parentheses to improve the readability of WHERE clauses that contain multiple, or compound, expressions, such as the following:

```
where (Continent = 'Africa' and Population gt 2000000) or
      (Continent = 'Asia' and Population gt 1000000)
```

△

Using Other Conditional Operators

You can use many different conditional operators in a WHERE clause. The following table lists other operators that you can use:

Table 2.4 Conditional Operators

Operator	Definition	Example
ANY	specifies that at least one of a set of values obtained from a subquery must satisfy a given condition	`where Population > any (select Population from sql.countries)`
ALL	specifies that all of the values obtained from a subquery must satisfy a given condition	`where Population > all (select Population from sql.countries)`
BETWEEN-AND	tests for values within an inclusive range	`where Population between 1000000 and 5000000`
CONTAINS	tests for values that contain a specified string	`where Continent contains 'America';`
EXISTS	tests for the existence of a set of values obtained from a subquery	`where exists (select * from sql.oilprod);`
IN	tests for values that match one of a list of values	`where Name in ('Africa', 'Asia');`
IS NULL or IS MISSING	tests for missing values	`where Population is missing;`

Operator	Definition	Example
LIKE	tests for values that match a specified pattern[1]	**where Continent like 'A%';**
=*	tests for values that sound like a specified value	**where Name =* 'Tiland';**

1 You can use a percent symbol (%) to match any number of characters. You can use an underscore (_) to match one arbitrary character.

Note: All of these operators can be prefixed with the NOT operator to form a negative condition. △

Using the IN Operator

The IN operator enables you to include values within a list that you supply. The following example uses the IN operator to include only the mountains and waterfalls in the SQL.FEATURES table:

```
proc sql outobs=12;
   title 'World Mountains and Waterfalls';
   select Name, Type, Height format=comma10.
      from sql.features
      where Type in ('Mountain', 'Waterfall')
      order by Height;
```

Output 2.26 Using the IN Operator

```
                    World Mountains and Waterfalls

               Name             Type           Height
               ------------------------------------------
               Niagara Falls    Waterfall         193
               Yosemite         Waterfall       2,425
               Tugela Falls     Waterfall       3,110
               Angel Falls      Waterfall       3,212
               Kosciusko        Mountain        7,310
               Pico Duarte      Mountain       10,417
               Cook             Mountain       12,349
               Matterhorn       Mountain       14,690
               Wilhelm          Mountain       14,793
               Mont Blanc       Mountain       15,771
               Ararat           Mountain       16,804
               Vinson Massif    Mountain       16,864
```

Using the IS MISSING Operator

The IS MISSING operator enables you to identify rows that contain columns with missing values. The following example selects countries that are not located on a continent; that is, these countries have a missing value in the Continent column:

```
proc sql;
   title 'Countries with Missing Continents';
   select Name, Continent
      from sql.countries
      where Continent is missing;
```

Note: The IS NULL operator is the same as, and interchangeable with, the IS MISSING operator. △

Output 2.27 Using the IS MISSING Operator

```
                        Countries with Missing Continents

        Name                                 Continent
        -----------------------------------------------------------------
        Bermuda
        Iceland
        Kalaallit Nunaat
```

Using the BETWEEN-AND Operators

To select rows based on a range of values, you can use the BETWEEN-AND operators. This example selects countries that have latitudes within five degrees of the Equator:

```
proc sql outobs=12;
   title 'Equatorial Cities of the World';
   select City, Country, Latitude
      from sql.worldcitycoords
      where Latitude between -5 and 5;
```

Note: In the tables used in these examples, latitude values that are south of the Equator are negative. Longitude values that are west of the Prime Meridian are also negative. △

Note: Because the BETWEEN-AND operators are inclusive, the values that you specify in the BETWEEN-AND expression are included in the results. △

Output 2.28 Using the BETWEEN-AND Operators

```
                    Equatorial Cities of the World

              City                 Country             Latitude
              ------------------------------------------------------
              Belem                Brazil                   -1
              Fortaleza            Brazil                   -4
              Bogota               Colombia                  4
              Cali                 Colombia                  3
              Brazzaville          Congo                    -4
              Quito                Ecuador                   0
              Cayenne              French Guiana             5
              Accra                Ghana                     5
              Medan                Indonesia                 3
              Palembang            Indonesia                -3
              Nairobi              Kenya                    -1
              Kuala Lumpur         Malaysia                  4
```

Using the LIKE Operator

The LIKE operator enables you to select rows based on pattern matching. For example, the following query returns all countries in the SQL.COUNTRIES table that begin with the letter *Z* and are any number of characters long, or end with the letter *a* and are five characters long:

```
proc sql;
   title1 'Country Names that Begin with the Letter "Z"';
   title2 'or Are 5 Characters Long and End with the Letter "a"';
   select Name
      from sql.countries
      where Name like 'Z%' or Name like '____a';
```

Output 2.29 Using the LIKE Operator

```
              Country Names that Begin with the Letter "Z"
           or Are 5 Characters Long and End with the Letter "a"

                   Name
                   ------------------------------------
                   China
                   Ghana
                   India
                   Kenya
                   Libya
                   Malta
                   Syria
                   Tonga
                   Zambia
                   Zimbabwe
```

The percent sign (%) and underscore (_) are wildcard characters. For more information about pattern matching with the LIKE comparison operator, see the "SQL Procedure" chapter in the *Base SAS Procedures Guide*.

Using Truncated String Comparison Operators

Truncated string comparison operators are used to compare two strings. They differ from conventional comparison operators in that, before executing the comparison, PROC SQL truncates the longer string to be the same length as the shorter string. The truncation is performed internally; neither operand is permanently changed. The following table lists the truncated comparison operators:

Table 2.5 Truncated String Comparison Operators

Symbol	Definition	Example
EQT	equal to truncated strings	`where Name eqt 'Aust';`
GTT	greater than truncated strings	`where Name gtt 'Bah';`
LTT	less than truncated strings	`where Name ltt 'An';`
GET	greater than or equal to truncated strings	`where Country get 'United A';`
LET	less than or equal to truncated strings	`where Lastname let 'Smith';`
NET	not equal to truncated strings	`where Style net 'TWO';`

The following example returns a list of U.S. states that have `'New '` at the beginning of their names:

```
proc sql;
   title '"New" U.S. States';
   select Name
      from sql.unitedstates
      where Name eqt 'New ';
```

Output 2.30 Using a Truncated String Comparison Operator

```
                    "New" U.S. States

          Name
          -----------------------------------
          New Hampshire
          New Jersey
          New Mexico
          New York
```

Using a WHERE Clause with Missing Values

If a column that you specify in a WHERE clause contains missing values, then a query might provide unexpected results. For example, the following query returns all features from the SQL.FEATURES table that have a depth of less than 500 feet:

```
/* incorrect output */

proc sql outobs=12;
   title 'World Features with a Depth of Less than 500 Feet';
```

```
select Name, Depth
   from sql.features
   where Depth lt 500
   order by Depth;
```

Output 2.31 Using a WHERE Clause with Missing Values (Incorrect Output)

```
              World Features with a Depth of Less than 500 Feet

                          Name                  Depth
                          ------------------------
                          Kalahari                .
                          Nile                    .
                          Citlaltepec             .
                          Lena                    .
                          Mont Blanc              .
                          Borneo                  .
                          Rub al Khali            .
                          Amur                    .
                          Yosemite                .
                          Cook                    .
                          Mackenzie-Peace         .
                          Mekong                  .
```

However, because PROC SQL treats missing values as smaller than nonmissing values, features that have no depth listed are also included in the results. To avoid this problem, you could adjust the WHERE expression to check for missing values and exclude them from the query results, as follows:

```
/* corrected output */

proc sql outobs=12;
   title 'World Features with a Depth of Less than 500 Feet';
   select Name, Depth
      from sql.features
      where Depth lt 500 and Depth is not missing
      order by Depth;
```

Output 2.32 Using a WHERE Clause with Missing Values (Corrected Output)

```
              World Features with a Depth of Less than 500 Feet

                          Name                  Depth
                          ------------------------
                          Baltic                  180
                          Aral Sea                222
                          Victoria                264
                          Hudson Bay              305
                          North                   308
```

Summarizing Data

You can use an *aggregate function* (or summary function) to produce a statistical summary of data in a table. The aggregate function instructs PROC SQL in how to combine data in one or more columns. If you specify one column as the argument to an aggregate function, then the values in that column are calculated. If you specify multiple arguments, then the arguments or columns that are listed are calculated.

Note: When more than one argument is used within an SQL aggregate function, the function is no longer considered to be an SQL aggregate or summary function. If there is a like-named Base SAS function, then PROC SQL executes the Base SAS function and the results that are returned are based on the values for the current row. If no like-named Base SAS function exists, then an error will occur. For example, if you use multiple arguments for the AVG function, an error will occur because there is no AVG function for Base SAS. △

When you use an aggregate function, PROC SQL applies the function to the entire table, unless you use a GROUP BY clause. You can use aggregate functions in the SELECT or HAVING clauses.

Note: See "Grouping Data" on page 47 for information about producing summaries of individual groups of data within a table. △

Using Aggregate Functions

The following table lists the aggregate functions that you can use:

Table 2.6 Aggregate Functions

Function	Definition
AVG, MEAN	mean or average of values
COUNT, FREQ, N	number of nonmissing values
CSS	corrected sum of squares
CV	coefficient of variation (percent)
MAX	largest value
MIN	smallest value
NMISS	number of missing values
PRT	probability of a greater absolute value of Student's t
RANGE	range of values
STD	standard deviation
STDERR	standard error of the mean
SUM	sum of values
SUMWGT	sum of the WEIGHT variable values[1]
T	Student's t value for testing the hypothesis that the population mean is zero

Function	Definition
USS	uncorrected sum of squares
VAR	variance

1 In the SQL procedure, each row has a weight of 1.

Note: You can use most other SAS functions in PROC SQL, but they are not treated as aggregate functions. △

Summarizing Data with a WHERE Clause

You can use aggregate, or summary functions, by using a WHERE clause. For a complete list of the aggregate functions that you can use, see Table 2.6 on page 40.

Using the MEAN Function with a WHERE Clause

This example uses the MEAN function to find the annual mean temperature for each country in the SQL.WORLDTEMPS table. The WHERE clause returns countries with a mean temperature that is greater than 75 degrees.

```
proc sql outobs=12;
   title 'Mean Temperatures for World Cities';
   select City, Country, mean(AvgHigh, AvgLow)
        as MeanTemp
     from sql.worldtemps
     where calculated MeanTemp gt 75
     order by MeanTemp desc;
```

Note: You must use the CALCULATED keyword to reference the calculated column. △

Output 2.33   Using the MEAN Function with a WHERE Clause

```
                    Mean Temperatures for World Cities

             City                 Country          MeanTemp
             ------------------------------------------------
             Lagos                Nigeria              82.5
             Manila               Philippines            82
             Bangkok              Thailand               82
             Singapore            Singapore              81
             Bombay               India                  79
             Kingston             Jamaica                78
             San Juan             Puerto Rico            78
             Calcutta             India                76.5
             Havana               Cuba                 76.5
             Nassau               Bahamas              76.5
```

Displaying Sums

The following example uses the SUM function to return the total oil reserves for all countries in the SQL.OILRSRVS table:

```
proc sql;
   title 'World Oil Reserves';
   select sum(Barrels) format=comma18. as TotalBarrels
      from sql.oilrsrvs;
```

Note: The SUM function produces a single row of output for the requested sum because no nonaggregate value appears in the SELECT clause. △

Output 2.34   Displaying Sums

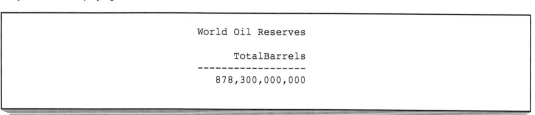

Combining Data from Multiple Rows into a Single Row

In the previous example, PROC SQL combined information from multiple rows of data into a single row of output. Specifically, the world oil reserves for each country were combined to form a total for all countries. Combining, or rolling up, of rows occurs when

□ the SELECT clause contains only columns that are specified within an aggregate function

□ the WHERE clause, if there is one, contains only columns that are specified in the SELECT clause.

Remerging Summary Statistics

The following example uses the MAX function to find the largest population in the SQL.COUNTRIES table and displays it in a column called MaxPopulation. Aggregate functions, such as the MAX function, can cause the same calculation to repeat for every row. This occurs whenever PROC SQL *remerges* data. Remerging occurs whenever any of the following conditions exist

□ The SELECT clause references a column that contains an aggregate function that is not listed in a GROUP BY clause.

□ The SELECT clause references a column that contains an aggregate function and other column or columns that are not listed in the GROUP BY clause.

□ One or more columns or column expressions that are listed in a HAVING clause are not included in a subquery or a GROUP BY clause.

In this example, PROC SQL writes the population of China, which is the largest population in the table:

```
proc sql outobs=12;
   title 'Largest Country Populations';
   select Name, Population format=comma20.,
          max(Population) as MaxPopulation format=comma20.
      from sql.countries
      order by Population desc;
```

Output 2.35 Using Aggregate Functions

```
                         Largest Country Populations

      Name                                 Population        MaxPopulation
      -------------------------------------------------------------------------
      China                             1,202,215,077        1,202,215,077
      India                               929,009,120        1,202,215,077
      United States                       263,294,808        1,202,215,077
      Indonesia                           202,393,859        1,202,215,077
      Brazil                              160,310,357        1,202,215,077
      Russia                              151,089,979        1,202,215,077
      Bangladesh                          126,387,850        1,202,215,077
      Japan                               126,345,434        1,202,215,077
      Pakistan                            123,062,252        1,202,215,077
      Nigeria                              99,062,003        1,202,215,077
      Mexico                               93,114,708        1,202,215,077
      Germany                              81,890,690        1,202,215,077
```

In some cases, you might need to use an aggregate function so that you can use its results in another calculation. To do this, you need only to construct one query for PROC SQL to automatically perform both calculations. This type of operation also causes PROC SQL to remerge the data.

For example, if you want to find the percentage of the total world population that resides in each country, then you construct a single query that

□ obtains the total world population by using the SUM function

□ divides each country's population by the total world population.

PROC SQL runs an internal query to find the sum and then runs another internal query to divide each country's population by the sum.

```
proc sql outobs=12;
   title 'Percentage of World Population in Countries';
   select Name, Population format=comma14.,
          (Population / sum(Population) * 100) as Percentage
          format=comma8.2
      from sql.countries
      order by Percentage desc;
```

Note: When a query remerges data, PROC SQL displays a note in the log to indicate that data remerging has occurred. △

Output 2.36 Remerging Summary Statistics

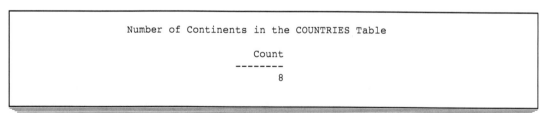

```
                 Percentage of World Population in Countries

        Name                                   Population  Percentage
        -----------------------------------------------------------------
        China                              1,202,215,077     20.88
        India                                929,009,120     16.13
        United States                        263,294,808      4.57
        Indonesia                            202,393,859      3.52
        Brazil                               160,310,357      2.78
        Russia                               151,089,979      2.62
        Bangladesh                           126,387,850      2.20
        Japan                                126,345,434      2.19
        Pakistan                             123,062,252      2.14
        Nigeria                               99,062,003      1.72
        Mexico                                93,114,708      1.62
        Germany                               81,890,690      1.42
```

Using Aggregate Functions with Unique Values

You can use DISTINCT with an aggregate function to cause the function to use only unique values from a column.

Counting Unique Values

The following query returns the number of distinct, nonmissing continents in the SQL.COUNTRIES table:

```
proc sql;
   title 'Number of Continents in the COUNTRIES Table';
   select count(distinct Continent) as Count
      from sql.countries;
```

Output 2.37 Using DISTINCT with the COUNT Function

```
              Number of Continents in the COUNTRIES Table

                               Count
                              --------
                                 8
```

Note: You cannot use **select count(distinct *)** to count distinct rows in a table. This code generates an error because PROC SQL does not know which duplicate column values to eliminate. △

Counting Nonmissing Values

Compare the previous example with the following query, which does not use the DISTINCT keyword. This query counts every nonmissing occurrence of a continent in the SQL.COUNTRIES table, including duplicate values:

```
proc sql;
   title 'Countries for Which a Continent is Listed';
   select count(Continent) as Count
      from sql.countries;
```

Output 2.38 Effect of Not Using DISTINCT with the COUNT Function

```
                    Countries for Which a Continent is Listed

                                    Count
                                  --------
                                     206
```

Counting All Rows

In the previous two examples, countries that have a missing value in the Continent column are ignored by the COUNT function. To obtain a count of all rows in the table, including countries that are not on a continent, you can use the following code in the SELECT clause:

```
proc sql;
   title 'Number of Countries in the SQL.COUNTRIES Table';
   select count(*) as Number
      from sql.countries;
```

Output 2.39 Using the COUNT Function to Count All Rows in a Table

```
                  Number of Countries in the SQL.COUNTRIES Table

                                   Number
                                 --------
                                    209
```

Summarizing Data with Missing Values

When you use an aggregate function with data that contains missing values, the results might not provide the information that you expect because many aggregate functions ignore missing values.

Finding Errors Caused by Missing Values

The AVG function returns the average of only the nonmissing values. The following query calculates the average length of three features in the SQL.FEATURES table: Angel Falls and the Amazon and Nile rivers:

```
/* incorrect output */

proc sql;
    title 'Average Length of Angel Falls, Amazon and Nile Rivers';
    select Name, Length, avg(Length) as AvgLength
       from sql.features
       where Name in ('Angel Falls', 'Amazon', 'Nile');
```

Output 2.40   Finding Errors Caused by Missing Values (Incorrect Output)

```
            Average Length of Angel Falls, Amazon and Nile Rivers

                Name              Length  AvgLength
                ------------------------------------
                Amazon              4000     4072.5
                Angel Falls            .     4072.5
                Nile                4145     4072.5
```

Because no length is stored for Angel Falls, the average includes only the Amazon and Nile rivers. The average is therefore incorrect.

Compare the result from the previous example with the following query, which includes a CASE expression to handle missing values:

```
/* corrected output */

proc sql;
    title 'Average Length of Angel Falls, Amazon and Nile Rivers';
    select Name, Length, case
                      when Length is missing then 0
                      else Length
                  end as NewLength,
           avg(calculated NewLength) as AvgLength
       from sql.features
       where Name in ('Angel Falls', 'Amazon', 'Nile');
```

Output 2.41   Finding Errors Caused by Missing Values (Corrected Output)

```
            Average Length of Angel Falls, Amazon and Nile Rivers

                Name            Length  NewLength  AvgLength
                ---------------------------------------------
                Amazon            4000       4000       2715
                Angel Falls          .          0       2715
                Nile              4145       4145       2715
```

Grouping Data

The GROUP BY clause groups data by a specified column or columns. When you use a GROUP BY clause, you also use an aggregate function in the SELECT clause or in a HAVING clause to instruct PROC SQL in how to summarize the data for each group. PROC SQL calculates the aggregate function separately for each group.

Grouping by One Column

The following example sums the populations of all countries to find the total population of each continent:

```
proc sql;
   title 'Total Populations of World Continents';
   select Continent, sum(Population) format=comma14. as TotalPopulation
      from sql.countries
      where Continent is not missing
      group by Continent;
```

Note: Countries for which a continent is not listed are excluded by the WHERE clause. △

Output 2.42 Grouping by One Column

```
              Total Populations of World Continents

                                               Total
           Continent                       Population
           -------------------------------------------------
           Africa                         710,529,592
           Asia                         3,381,858,879
           Australia                       18,255,944
           Central America and Caribbean   66,815,930
           Europe                         872,192,202
           North America                 384,801,818
           Oceania                          5,342,368
           South America                 317,568,801
```

Grouping without Summarizing

When you use a GROUP BY clause without an aggregate function, PROC SQL treats the GROUP BY clause as if it were an ORDER BY clause and displays a message in the log that informs you that this has happened. The following example attempts to group high and low temperature information for each city in the SQL.WORLDTEMPS table by country:

```
proc sql outobs=12;
   title 'High and Low Temperatures';
   select City, Country, AvgHigh, AvgLow
      from sql.worldtemps
      group by Country;
```

The output and log show that PROC SQL transforms the GROUP BY clause into an ORDER BY clause.

Output 2.43 Grouping without Aggregate Functions

```
                         High and Low Temperatures

        City               Country          AvgHigh    AvgLow
        -----------------------------------------------------------
        Algiers            Algeria             90         45
        Buenos Aires       Argentina           87         48
        Sydney             Australia           79         44
        Vienna             Austria             76         28
        Nassau             Bahamas             88         65
        Hamilton           Bermuda             85         59
        Sao Paulo          Brazil              81         53
        Rio de Janeiro     Brazil              85         64
        Quebec             Canada              76          5
        Montreal           Canada              77          8
        Toronto            Canada              80         17
        Beijing            China               86         17
```

Output 2.44 Grouping without Aggregate Functions (Partial Log)

```
   WARNING: A GROUP BY clause has been transformed into an ORDER BY clause because
            neither the SELECT clause nor the optional HAVING clause of the
            associated table-expression referenced a summary function.
```

Grouping by Multiple Columns

To group by multiple columns, separate the column names with commas within the GROUP BY clause. You can use aggregate functions with any of the columns that you select. The following example groups by both Location and Type, producing total square miles for the deserts and lakes in each location in the SQL.FEATURES table:

```
proc sql;
   title 'Total Square Miles of Deserts and Lakes';
   select Location, Type, sum(Area) as TotalArea format=comma16.
      from sql.features
      where type in ('Desert', 'Lake')
      group by Location, Type;
```

Output 2.45 Grouping by Multiple Columns

```
                    Total Square Miles of Deserts and Lakes

          Location             Type             TotalArea
          ------------------------------------------------------
          Africa               Desert           3,725,000
          Africa               Lake                50,958
          Asia                 Lake                25,300
          Australia            Desert             300,000
          Canada               Lake                12,275
          China                Desert             500,000
          Europe - Asia        Lake               143,550
          North America        Desert             140,000
          North America        Lake                77,200
          Russia               Lake                11,780
          Saudi Arabia         Desert             250,000
```

Grouping and Sorting Data

You can order grouped results with an ORDER BY clause. The following example takes the previous example and adds an ORDER BY clause to change the order of the Location column from ascending order to descending order:

```
proc sql;
   title 'Total Square Miles of Deserts and Lakes';
   select Location, Type, sum(Area) as TotalArea format=comma16.
      from sql.features
      where type in ('Desert', 'Lake')
      group by Location, Type
      order by Location desc;
```

Output 2.46 Grouping with an ORDER BY Clause

```
                    Total Square Miles of Deserts and Lakes

          Location             Type             TotalArea
          ------------------------------------------------------
          Saudi Arabia         Desert             250,000
          Russia               Lake                11,780
          North America        Lake                77,200
          North America        Desert             140,000
          Europe - Asia        Lake               143,550
          China                Desert             500,000
          Canada               Lake                12,275
          Australia            Desert             300,000
          Asia                 Lake                25,300
          Africa               Desert           3,725,000
          Africa               Lake                50,958
```

Grouping with Missing Values

When a column contains missing values, PROC SQL treats the missing values as a single group. This can sometimes provide unexpected results.

Finding Grouping Errors Caused by Missing Values

In this example, because the SQL.COUNTRIES table contains some missing values in the Continent column, the missing values combine to form a single group that has the total area of the countries that have a missing value in the Continent column:

```
/* incorrect output */

proc sql outobs=12;
   title 'Areas of World Continents';
   select Name format=$25.,
          Continent,
          sum(Area) format=comma12. as TotalArea
      from sql.countries
      group by Continent
      order by Continent, Name;
```

The output is incorrect because Bermuda, Iceland, and Kalaallit Nunaat are not actually part of the same continent; however, PROC SQL treats them that way because they all have a missing character value in the Continent column.

Output 2.47   Finding Grouping Errors Caused by Missing Values (Incorrect Output)

```
                            Areas of World Continents

        Name                         Continent                      TotalArea
        -------------------------------------------------------------------------
        Bermuda                                                        876,800
        Iceland                                                        876,800
        Kalaallit Nunaat                                               876,800
        Algeria                      Africa                         11,299,595
        Angola                       Africa                         11,299,595
        Benin                        Africa                         11,299,595
        Botswana                     Africa                         11,299,595
        Burkina Faso                 Africa                         11,299,595
        Burundi                      Africa                         11,299,595
        Cameroon                     Africa                         11,299,595
        Cape Verde                   Africa                         11,299,595
        Central African  Republic    Africa                         11,299,595
```

To correct the query from the previous example, you can write a WHERE clause to exclude the missing values from the results:

```
/* corrected output */

proc sql outobs=12;
   title 'Areas of World Continents';
   select Name format=$25.,
          Continent,
```

```
         sum(Area) format=comma12. as TotalArea
    from sql.countries
    where Continent is not missing
    group by Continent
    order by Continent, Name;
```

Output 2.48 Adjusting the Query to Avoid Errors Due to Missing Values (Corrected Output)

```
                          Areas of World Continents

    Name                           Continent                       TotalArea
    --------------------------------------------------------------------------
    Algeria                        Africa                         11,299,595
    Angola                         Africa                         11,299,595
    Benin                          Africa                         11,299,595
    Botswana                       Africa                         11,299,595
    Burkina Faso                   Africa                         11,299,595
    Burundi                        Africa                         11,299,595
    Cameroon                       Africa                         11,299,595
    Cape Verde                     Africa                         11,299,595
    Central African  Republic      Africa                         11,299,595
    Chad                           Africa                         11,299,595
    Comoros                        Africa                         11,299,595
    Congo                          Africa                         11,299,595
```

Note: Aggregate functions, such as the SUM function, can cause the same calculation to repeat for every row. This occurs whenever PROC SQL remerges data. See "Remerging Summary Statistics" on page 42 for more information about remerging. △

Filtering Grouped Data

You can use a HAVING clause with a GROUP BY clause to filter grouped data. The HAVING clause affects groups in a way that is similar to the way in which a WHERE clause affects individual rows. When you use a HAVING clause, PROC SQL displays only the groups that satisfy the HAVING expression.

Using a Simple HAVING Clause

The following example groups the features in the SQL.FEATURES table by type and then displays only the numbers of islands, oceans, and seas:

```
proc sql;
    title 'Numbers of Islands, Oceans, and Seas';
    select Type, count(*) as Number
        from sql.features
        group by Type
        having Type in ('Island', 'Ocean', 'Sea')
        order by Type;
```

Output 2.49   Using a Simple HAVING Clause

```
                    Numbers of Islands, Oceans, and Seas

                         Type          Number
                         --------------------
                         Island             6
                         Ocean              4
                         Sea               13
```

Choosing between HAVING and WHERE

The differences between the HAVING clause and the WHERE clause are shown in the following table. Because you use the HAVING clause when you work with groups of data, queries that contain a HAVING clause usually also contain the following:

☐ a GROUP BY clause

☐ an aggregate function.

Note: When you use a HAVING clause without a GROUP BY clause, PROC SQL treats the HAVING clause as if it were a WHERE clause and provides a message in the log that informs you that this occurred. △

Table 2.7   Differences between the HAVING Clause and WHERE Clause

HAVING clause attributes	WHERE clause attributes
is typically used to specify conditions for including or excluding groups of rows from a table.	is used to specify conditions for including or excluding individual rows from a table.
must follow the GROUP BY clause in a query, if used with a GROUP BY clause.	must precede the GROUP BY clause in a query, if used with a GROUP BY clause.
is affected by a GROUP BY clause; when there is no GROUP BY clause, the HAVING clause is treated like a WHERE clause.	is not affected by a GROUP BY clause.
is processed after the GROUP BY clause and any aggregate functions.	is processed before a GROUP BY clause, if there is one, and before any aggregate functions.

Using HAVING with Aggregate Functions

The following query returns the populations of all continents that have more than 15 countries:

```
proc sql;
   title 'Total Populations of Continents with More than 15 Countries';
   select Continent,
          sum(Population) as TotalPopulation format=comma16.,
          count(*) as Count
      from sql.countries
      group by Continent
      having count(*) gt 15
      order by Continent;
```

The HAVING expression contains the COUNT function, which counts the number of rows within each group.

Output 2.50   Using HAVING with the COUNT Function

```
          Total Populations of Continents with More than 15 Countries

          Continent                        TotalPopulation    Count
          ------------------------------------------------------------
          Africa                               710,529,592       53
          Asia                               3,381,858,879       48
          Central America and Caribbean         66,815,930       25
          Europe                               813,481,724       51
```

Validating a Query

The VALIDATE statement enables you to check the syntax of a query for correctness without submitting it to PROC SQL. PROC SQL displays a message in the log to indicate whether the syntax is correct.

```
proc sql;
   validate
      select Name, Statehood
         from sql.unitedstates
         where Statehood lt '01Jan1800'd;
```

Output 2.51   Validating a Query (Partial Log)

```
3  proc sql;
4     validate
5        select Name, Statehood
6           from sql.unitedstates
7           where Statehood lt '01Jan1800'd;
NOTE: PROC SQL statement has valid syntax.
```

The following example shows an invalid query and the corresponding log message:

```
proc sql;
   validate
       select Name, Statehood
       from sql.unitedstates
       where lt '01Jan1800'd;
```

Output 2.52   Validating an Invalid Query (Partial Log)

```
3   proc sql;
4      validate
5         select Name, Statehood
6         from sql.unitedstates
7         where lt '01Jan1800'd;
                 ------------
                     22
                     76
ERROR 22-322: Syntax error, expecting one of the following: !, !!, &, *, **,
              +, -, /, <, <=, <>, =, >, >=, ?, AND, CONTAINS, EQ, GE, GROUP,
              GT, HAVING, LE, LIKE, LT, NE, OR, ORDER, ^=, |, ||, ~=.

ERROR 76-322: Syntax error, statement will be ignored.

NOTE: The SAS System stopped processing this step because of errors.
```

CHAPTER

CHAPTER

3

Retrieving Data from Multiple Tables

Introduction **56**
Selecting Data from More Than One Table by Using Joins **56**
    Inner Joins **57**
        Using Table Aliases **58**
        Specifying the Order of Join Output **59**
        Creating Inner Joins Using INNER JOIN Keywords **59**
        Joining Tables Using Comparison Operators **59**
        The Effects of Null Values on Joins **60**
        Creating Multicolumn Joins **62**
        Selecting Data from More Than Two Tables **63**
        Showing Relationships within a Single Table Using Self-Joins **64**
    Outer Joins **65**
        Including Nonmatching Rows with the Left Outer Join **65**
        Including Nonmatching Rows with the Right Outer Join **66**
        Selecting All Rows with the Full Outer Join **67**
    Specialty Joins **68**
        Including All Combinations of Rows with the Cross Join **68**
        Including All Rows with the Union Join **69**
        Matching Rows with a Natural Join **69**
    Using the Coalesce Function in Joins **70**
    Comparing DATA Step Match-Merges with PROC SQL Joins **71**
        When All of the Values Match **71**
        When Only Some of the Values Match **72**
        When the Position of the Values Is Important **73**
Using Subqueries to Select Data **74**
    Single-Value Subqueries **75**
    Multiple-Value Subqueries **75**
    Correlated Subqueries **76**
    Testing for the Existence of a Group of Values **77**
    Multiple Levels of Subquery Nesting **78**
    Combining a Join with a Subquery **79**
When to Use Joins and Subqueries **80**
Combining Queries with Set Operators **81**
    Working with Two or More Query Results **81**
    Producing Unique Rows from Both Queries (UNION) **82**
    Producing Rows That Are in Only the First Query Result (EXCEPT) **83**
    Producing Rows That Belong to Both Query Results (INTERSECT) **84**
    Concatenating Query Results (OUTER UNION) **85**
    Producing Rows from the First Query or the Second Query **86**

Introduction

This chapter shows you how to

☐ select data from more than one table by joining the tables together

☐ use subqueries to select data from one table based on data values from another table

☐ combine the results of more than one query by using set operators.

Note: Unless otherwise noted, the PROC SQL operations that are shown in this chapter apply to views as well as tables. For more information about views, see Chapter 4, "Creating and Updating Tables and Views," on page 89. △

Selecting Data from More Than One Table by Using Joins

The data that you need for a report could be located in more than one table. In order to select the data from the tables, *join* the tables in a query. Joining tables enables you to select data from multiple tables as if the data were contained in one table. Joins do not alter the original tables.

The most basic type of join is simply two tables that are listed in the FROM clause of a SELECT statement. The following query joins the two tables that are shown in Output 3.1 and creates Output 3.2.

```
proc sql;
    title 'Table One and Table Two';
    select *
        from one, two;
```

Output 3.1   Table One and Table Two

```
                          Table One

                           X   Y
                      ------------------
                           1   2
                           2   3
```

```
                          Table Two

                           X   Z
                      ------------------
                           2   5
                           3   6
                           4   9
```

Output 3.2   Cartesian Product of Table One and Table Two

```
                    Table One and Table Two

                    X   Y            X   Z
          ---------------------------------------
                    1   2            2   5
                    1   2            3   6
                    1   2            4   9
                    2   3            2   5
                    2   3            3   6
                    2   3            4   9
```

Joining tables in this way returns the *Cartesian product* of the tables. Each row from the first table is combined with every row from the second table. When you run this query, the following message is written to the SAS log:

Output 3.3   Cartesian Product Log Message

```
NOTE: The execution of this query involves performing one or more Cartesian
      product joins that can not be optimized.
```

The Cartesian product of large tables can be huge. Typically, you want a subset of the Cartesian product. You specify the subset by declaring the join type.

There are two types of joins:

- □ *Inner Joins* return a result table for all the rows in a table that have one or more matching rows in the other table or tables that are listed in the FROM clause.

- □ *Outer Joins* are inner joins that are augmented with rows that did not match with any row from the other table in the join. There are three kinds of outer joins: left, right, and full.

Inner Joins

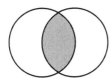

An inner join returns only the subset of rows from the first table that matches rows from the second table. You can specify the columns that you want to be compared for matching values in a WHERE clause.

The following code adds a WHERE clause to the previous query. The WHERE clause specifies that only rows whose values in column X of Table One match values in column X of Table Two should appear in the output. Compare this query's output to Output 3.2.

```
proc sql;
   select * from one, two
      where one.x=two.x;
```

Output 3.4   Table One and Table Two Joined

```
                        Table One and Table Two

               X   Y               X   Z
        ----------------------------------------
               2   3               2   5
```

The output contains only one row because only one value in column X matches from each table. In an inner join, only the matching rows are selected. Outer joins can return nonmatching rows; they are covered in "Outer Joins" on page 65.

Note that the column names in the WHERE clause are prefixed by their table names. This is known as *qualifying* the column names, and it is necessary when you specify columns that have the same name from more than one table. Qualifying the column name avoids creating an ambiguous column reference.

Using Table Aliases

A table *alias* is a temporary, alternate name for a table. You specify table aliases in the FROM clause. Table aliases are used in joins to qualify column names and can make a query easier to read by abbreviating table names.

The following example compares the oil production of countries to their oil reserves by joining the OILPROD and OILRSRVS tables on their Country columns. Because the Country columns are common to both tables, they are qualified with their table aliases. You could also qualify the columns by prefixing the column names with the table names.

Note: The AS keyword is optional. △

```
proc sql outobs=6;
   title 'Oil Production/Reserves of Countries';
   select * from sql.oilprod as p, sql.oilrsrvs as r
      where p.country = r.country;
```

Output 3.5   Abbreviating Column Names by Using Table Aliases

```
                    Oil Production/Reserves of Countries

                        Barrels
        Country         PerDay  Country                    Barrels
        ------------------------------------------------------------------
        Algeria       1,400,000 Algeria              9,200,000,000
        Canada        2,500,000 Canada               7,000,000,000
        China         3,000,000 China               25,000,000,000
        Egypt           900,000 Egypt                4,000,000,000
        Indonesia     1,500,000 Indonesia            5,000,000,000
        Iran          4,000,000 Iran                90,000,000,000
```

Note that each table's Country column is displayed. Typically, once you have determined that a join is functioning correctly, you include just one of the matching columns in the SELECT clause.

Specifying the Order of Join Output

You can order the output of joined tables by one or more columns from either table. The next example's output is ordered in descending order by the BarrelsPerDay column. It is not necessary to qualify BarrelsPerDay, because the column exists only in the OILPROD table.

```
proc sql outobs=6;
   title 'Oil Production/Reserves of Countries';
   select p.country, barrelsperday 'Production', barrels 'Reserves'
      from sql.oilprod p, sql.oilrsrvs r
      where p.country = r.country
      order by barrelsperday desc;
```

Output 3.6 Ordering the Output of Joined Tables

```
                 Oil Production/Reserves of Countries

      Country                       Production          Reserves
      ------------------------------------------------------------
      Saudi Arabia                  9,000,000     260,000,000,000
      United States of America      8,000,000      30,000,000,000
      Iran                          4,000,000      90,000,000,000
      Norway                        3,500,000      11,000,000,000
      Mexico                        3,400,000      50,000,000,000
      China                         3,000,000      25,000,000,000
```

Creating Inner Joins Using INNER JOIN Keywords

The INNER JOIN keywords can be used to join tables. The ON clause replaces the WHERE clause for specifying columns to join. PROC SQL provides these keywords primarily for compatibility with the other joins (OUTER, RIGHT, and LEFT JOIN). Using INNER JOIN with an ON clause provides the same functionality as listing tables in the FROM clause and specifying join columns with a WHERE clause.

This code produces the same output as the previous code but uses the INNER JOIN construction.

```
proc sql ;
   select p.country, barrelsperday 'Production', barrels 'Reserves'
      from sql.oilprod p inner join sql.oilrsrvs r
          on p.country = r.country
   order by barrelsperday desc;
```

Joining Tables Using Comparison Operators

Tables can be joined by using comparison operators other than the equal sign (=) in the WHERE clause (for a list of comparison operators, see "Retrieving Rows Based on a Comparison" on page 32). In this example, all U.S. cities in the USCITYCOORDS table are selected that are south of Cairo, Egypt. The compound WHERE clause specifies the city of Cairo in the WORLDCITYCOORDS table and joins USCITYCOORDS and WORLDCITYCOORDS on their Latitude columns, using a less-than (**lt**) operator.

```
proc sql;
   title 'US Cities South of Cairo, Egypt';
   select us.City, us.State, us.Latitude, world.city, world.latitude
      from sql.worldcitycoords world, sql.uscitycoords us
```

```
    where world.city = 'Cairo' and
          us.latitude lt world.latitude;
```

Output 3.7   Using Comparison Operators to Join Tables

```
                         US Cities South of Cairo, Egypt

          City              State  Latitude  City                      Latitude
          -------------------------------------------------------------------------
          Honolulu          HI          21  Cairo                           30
          Key West          FL          24  Cairo                           30
          Miami             FL          26  Cairo                           30
          San Antonio       TX          29  Cairo                           30
          Tampa             FL          28  Cairo                           30
```

When you run this query, the following message is written to the SAS log:

Output 3.8   Comparison Query Log Message

```
    NOTE: The execution of this query involves performing one or more Cartesian
          product joins that can not be optimized.
```

Recall that you see this message when you run a query that joins tables without specifying matching columns in a WHERE clause. PROC SQL also displays this message whenever tables are joined by using an inequality operator.

The Effects of Null Values on Joins

Most database products treat nulls as distinct entities and do not match them in joins. PROC SQL treats nulls as missing values and as matches for joins. Any null will match with any other null of the same type (character or numeric) in a join.

The following example joins Table One and Table Two on column B. There are null values in column B of both tables. Notice in the output that the null value in row c of Table One matches all the null values in Table Two. This is probably not the intended result for the join.

```
proc sql;
    title 'One and Two Joined';
    select one.a 'One', one.b, two.a 'Two', two.b
      from one, two
      where one.b=two.b;
```

Output 3.9 Joining Tables That Contain Null Values

```
                          Table One

                    a                 b
                    ------------------
                    a                 1
                    b                 2
                    c                 .
                    d                 4
```

```
                          Table Two

                    a                 b
                    ------------------
                    a                 1
                    b                 2
                    c                 .
                    d                 4
                    e                 .
                    f                 .
```

```
                     One and Two Joined

              One            b  Two            b
              ------------------------------------
              a              1  a              1
              b              2  b              2
              c              .  c              .
              d              4  d              4
              c              .  e              .
              c              .  f              .
```

In order to specify only the nonmissing values for the join, use the IS NOT MISSING operator:

```
proc sql;
   select one.a 'One', one.b, two.a 'Two', two.b
      from one, two
      where one.b=two.b and
            one.b is not missing;
```

Output 3.10 Results of Adding IS NOT MISSING to Joining Tables That Contain Null Values

```
                     One and Two Joined

              One            b  Two            b
              ------------------------------------
              a              1  a              1
              b              2  b              2
              d              4  d              4
```

Creating Multicolumn Joins

When a row is distinguished by a combination of values in more than one column, use all the necessary columns in the join. For example, a city name could exist in more than one country. To select the correct city, you must specify both the city and country columns in the joining query's WHERE clause.

This example displays the latitude and longitude of capital cities by joining the COUNTRIES table with the WORLDCITYCOORDS table. To minimize the number of rows in the example output, the first part of the WHERE expression selects capitals with names that begin with the letter *L* from the COUNTRIES table.

```
proc sql;
   title 'Coordinates of Capital Cities';
   select Capital format=$12., Name format=$12.,
          City format=$12., Country format=$12.,
          Latitude, Longitude
      from sql.countries, sql.worldcitycoords
      where Capital like 'L%' and
                Capital = City;
```

London occurs once as a capital city in the COUNTRIES table. However, in WORLDCITYCOORDS, London is found twice: as a city in England and again as a city in Canada. Specifying only `Capital = City` in the WHERE expression yields the following incorrect output:

Output 3.11   Selecting Capital City Coordinates (incorrect output)

```
                    Coordinates of Capital Cities

   Capital      Name         City         Country      Latitude  Longitude
   -------------------------------------------------------------------------
   La Paz       Bolivia      La Paz       Bolivia         -16        -69
   London       England      London       Canada           43        -81
   Lima         Peru         Lima         Peru            -13        -77
   Lisbon       Portugal     Lisbon       Portugal         39        -10
   London       England      London       England          51          0
```

Notice in the output that the inner join incorrectly matches London, England, to both London, Canada, and London, England. By also joining the country name columns together (COUNTRIES.Name to WORLDCITYCOORDS.Country), the rows match correctly.

```
proc sql;
   title 'Coordinates of Capital Cities';
   select Capital format=$12., Name format=$12.,
          City format=$12., Country format=$12.,
          latitude, longitude
      from sql.countries, sql.worldcitycoords
      where Capital like 'L%' and
            Capital = City and
            Name = Country;
```

Output 3.12 Selecting Capital City Coordinates (correct output)

```
                       Coordinates of Capital Cities

      Capital      Name         City         Country      Latitude  Longitude
      -------------------------------------------------------------------------
      La Paz       Bolivia      La Paz       Bolivia           -16        -69
      Lima         Peru         Lima         Peru              -13        -77
      Lisbon       Portugal     Lisbon       Portugal           39        -10
      London       England      London       England            51          0
```

Selecting Data from More Than Two Tables

The data that you need could be located in more than two tables. For example, if you want to show the coordinates of the capitals of the states in the United States, then you need to join the UNITEDSTATES table, which contains the state capitals, with the USCITYCOORDS table, which contains the coordinates of cities in the United States. Because cities must be joined along with their states for an accurate join (similarly to the previous example), you must join the tables on both the city and state columns of the tables.

Joining the cities, by joining the UNITEDSTATES.Capital column to the USCITYCOORDS.City column, is straightforward. However, in the UNITEDSTATES table the Name column contains the full state name, while in USCITYCOORDS the states are specified by their postal code. It is therefore impossible to directly join the two tables on their state columns. To solve this problem, it is necessary to use the POSTALCODES table, which contains both the state names and their postal codes, as an intermediate table to make the correct relationship between UNITEDSTATES and USCITYCOORDS. The correct solution joins the UNITEDSTATES.Name column to the POSTALCODES.Name column (matching the full state names), and the POSTALCODES.Code column to the USCITYCOORDS.State column (matching the state postal codes).

```
title 'Coordinates of State Capitals';
proc sql outobs=10;
   select us.Capital format=$15., us.Name 'State' format=$15.,
          pc.Code, c.Latitude, c.Longitude
      from sql.unitedstates us, sql.postalcodes pc,
          sql.uscitycoords c
      where us.Capital = c.City and
          us.Name = pc.Name and
          pc.Code = c.State;
```

Output 3.13   Selecting Data from More Than Two Tables

```
                      Coordinates of State Capitals

      Capital         State            Code  Latitude  Longitude
      -----------------------------------------------------------
      Albany          New York         NY        43       -74
      Annapolis       Maryland         MD        39       -77
      Atlanta         Georgia          GA        34       -84
      Augusta         Maine            ME        44       -70
      Austin          Texas            TX        30       -98
      Baton Rouge     Louisiana        LA        31       -91
      Bismarck        North Dakota     ND        47      -101
      Boise           Idaho            ID        43      -116
      Boston          Massachusetts    MA        42       -72
      Carson City     Nevada           NV        39      -120
```

Showing Relationships within a Single Table Using Self-Joins

When you need to show comparative relationships between values in a table, it is sometimes necessary to join columns within the same table. Joining a table to itself is called a *self-join*, or *reflexive join*. You can think of a self-join as PROC SQL making an internal copy of a table and joining the table to its copy.

For example, the following code uses a self-join to select cities that have average yearly high temperatures equal to the average yearly low temperatures of other cities.

```
proc sql;
   title "Cities' High Temps = Cities' Low Temps";
   select High.City format $12., High.Country format $12.,
          High.AvgHigh, ' | ',
          Low.City format $12., Low.Country format $12.,
          Low.AvgLow
      from sql.worldtemps High, sql.worldtemps Low
      where High.AvgHigh = Low.AvgLow and
            High.city ne Low.city and
            High.country ne Low.country;
```

Notice that the WORLDTEMPS table is assigned two aliases, **High** and **Low**. Conceptually, this makes a copy of the table so that a join can be made between the table and its copy. The WHERE clause selects those rows that have high temperature equal to low temperature.

The WHERE clause also prevents a city from being joined to itself (**City ne City** and **Country ne Country**), although, in this case, it is highly unlikely that the high temperature would be equal to the low temperature for the same city.

Output 3.14 Joining a Table to Itself (Self-Join)

```
                        Cities' High Temps = Cities' Low Temps

City            Country         AvgHigh     City          Country         AvgLow
------------------------------------------------------------------------------------
Amsterdam       Netherlands         70   |  San Juan      Puerto Rico         70
Auckland        New Zealand         75   |  Lagos         Nigeria             75
Auckland        New Zealand         75   |  Manila        Philippines         75
Berlin          Germany             75   |  Lagos         Nigeria             75
Berlin          Germany             75   |  Manila        Philippines         75
Bogota          Colombia            69   |  Bangkok       Thailand            69
Cape Town       South Africa        70   |  San Juan      Puerto Rico         70
Copenhagen      Denmark             73   |  Singapore     Singapore           73
Dublin          Ireland             68   |  Bombay        India               68
Glasgow         Scotland            65   |  Nassau        Bahamas             65
London          England             73   |  Singapore     Singapore           73
Oslo            Norway              73   |  Singapore     Singapore           73
Reykjavik       Iceland             57   |  Caracas       Venezuela           57
Stockholm       Sweden              70   |  San Juan      Puerto Rico         70
```

Outer Joins

Outer joins are inner joins that are augmented with rows from one table that do not match any row from the other table in the join. The resulting output includes rows that match and rows that do not match from the join's source tables. Nonmatching rows have null values in the columns from the unmatched table. Use the ON clause instead of the WHERE clause to specify the column or columns on which you are joining the tables. However, you can continue to use the WHERE clause to subset the query result.

Including Nonmatching Rows with the Left Outer Join

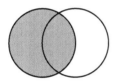

A left outer join lists matching rows and rows from the left-hand table (the first table listed in the FROM clause) that do not match any row in the right-hand table. A left join is specified with the keywords LEFT JOIN and ON.

For example, to list the coordinates of the capitals of international cities, join the COUNTRIES table, which contains capitals, with the WORLDCITYCOORDS table, which contains cities' coordinates, by using a left join. The left join lists all capitals, regardless of whether the cities exist in WORLDCITYCOORDS. Using an inner join would list only capital cities for which there is a matching city in WORLDCITYCOORDS.

```
proc sql outobs=10;
   title 'Coordinates of Capital Cities';
   select Capital format=$20., Name 'Country' format=$20.,
          Latitude, Longitude
      from sql.countries a left join sql.worldcitycoords b
         on a.Capital = b.City and
            a.Name = b.Country
      order by Capital;
```

Output 3.15   Left Join of COUNTRIES and WORLDCITYCOORDS

```
                        Coordinates of Capital Cities

           Capital              Country              Latitude  Longitude
           -----------------------------------------------------------------
                                Channel Islands         .          .
           Abu Dhabi            United Arab Emirates     .          .
           Abuja                Nigeria                  .          .
           Accra                Ghana                    5          0
           Addis Ababa          Ethiopia                 9          39
           Algiers              Algeria                 37          3
           Almaty               Kazakhstan               .          .
           Amman                Jordan                  32          36
           Amsterdam            Netherlands             52          5
           Andorra la Vella     Andorra                  .          .
```

Including Nonmatching Rows with the Right Outer Join

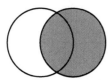

A right join, specified with the keywords RIGHT JOIN and ON, is the opposite of a left join: nonmatching rows from the right-hand table (the second table listed in the FROM clause) are included with all matching rows in the output. This example reverses the join of the last example; it uses a right join to select all the cities from the WORLDCITYCOORDS table and displays the population only if the city is the capital of a country (that is, if the city exists in the COUNTRIES table).

```
proc sql outobs=10;
   title 'Populations of Capitals Only';
   select City format=$20., Country 'Country' format=$20.,
          Population
      from sql.countries right join sql.worldcitycoords
           on Capital = City and
              Name = Country
      order by City;
```

Output 3.16 Right Join of COUNTRIES and WORLDCITYCOORDS

```
                       Populations of Capitals Only

         City                    Country              Population
         ------------------------------------------------------------
         Abadan                  Iran                          .
         Acapulco                Mexico                        .
         Accra                   Ghana                  17395511
         Adana                   Turkey                        .
         Addis Ababa             Ethiopia               59291170
         Adelaide                Australia                     .
         Aden                    Yemen                         .
         Ahmenabad               India                         .
         Algiers                 Algeria                28171132
         Alice Springs           Australia                     .
```

Selecting All Rows with the Full Outer Join

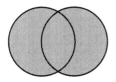

A full outer join, specified with the keywords FULL JOIN and ON, selects all matching and nonmatching rows. This example displays the first ten matching and nonmatching rows from the City and Capital columns of WORLDCITYCOORDS and COUNTRIES. Note that the pound sign (#) is used as a line split character in the labels.

```
proc sql outobs=10;
   title 'Populations and/or Coordinates of World Cities';
   select City '#City#(WORLDCITYCOORDS)' format=$20.,
          Capital '#Capital#(COUNTRIES)' format=$20.,
          Population, Latitude, Longitude
      from sql.countries full join sql.worldcitycoords
         on Capital = City and
            Name = Country;
```

Output 3.17 Full Outer Join of COUNTRIES and WORLDCITYCOORDS

```
               Populations and/or Coordinates of World Cities

   City                    Capital
   (WORLDCITYCOORDS)       (COUNTRIES)        Population  Latitude  Longitude
   ---------------------------------------------------------------------------
                                                 146436         .          .
   Abadan                                             .        30         48
                           Abu Dhabi             2818628         .          .
                           Abuja                99062003         .          .
   Acapulco                                           .        17       -100
   Accra                   Accra                17395511         5          0
   Adana                                              .        37         35
   Addis Ababa             Addis Ababa          59291170         9         39
   Adelaide                                           .       -35        138
   Aden                                               .        13         45
```

Specialty Joins

Three types of joins—cross joins, union joins, and natural joins—are special cases of the standard join types.

Including All Combinations of Rows with the Cross Join

A cross join is a Cartesian product; it returns the product of two tables. Like a Cartesian product, a cross join's output can be limited by a WHERE clause.

This example shows a cross join of the tables One and Two:

Output 3.18   Tables One and Two

```
                           Table One

                            X   Y
                       ------------------
                            1   2
                            2   3
```

```
                           Table Two

                            W   Z
                       ------------------
                            2   5
                            3   6
                            4   9
```

```
proc sql;
   select *
      from one cross join two;
```

Output 3.19   Cross Join

```
                        The SAS System

                   X   Y              W   Z
              ------------------------------------
                   1   2              2   5
                   1   2              3   6
                   1   2              4   9
                   2   3              2   5
                   2   3              3   6
                   2   3              4   9
```

Like a conventional Cartesian product, a cross join causes a note regarding Cartesian products in the SAS log.

Including All Rows with the Union Join

A union join combines two tables without attempting to match rows. All columns and rows from both tables are included. Combining tables with a union join is similar to combining them with the OUTER UNION set operator (see "Combining Queries with Set Operators" on page 81). A union join's output can be limited by a WHERE clause.

This example shows a union join of the same One and Two tables that were used earlier to demonstrate a cross join:

```
proc sql;
   select *
      from one union join two;
```

Output 3.20 Union Join

```
                      X   Y              W   Z
          -------------------------------------------
                      .                  2   5
                      .                  3   6
                      .                  4   9
                      1   2              .
                      2   3              .
```

Matching Rows with a Natural Join

A natural join automatically selects columns from each table to use in determining matching rows. With a natural join, PROC SQL identifies columns in each table that have the same name and type; rows in which the values of these columns are equal are returned as matching rows. The ON clause is implied.

This example produces the same results as the example in "Specifying the Order of Join Output" on page 59:

```
proc sql outobs=6;
   title 'Oil Production/Reserves of Countries';
   select country, barrelsperday 'Production', barrels 'Reserve'
      from sql.oilprod natural join sql.oilrsrvs
      order by barrelsperday desc;
```

Output 3.21 Natural Inner Join of OILPROD and OILRSRVS

```
                    Oil Production/Reserves of Countries

        Country                      Production          Reserve
        -----------------------------------------------------------
        Saudi Arabia                  9,000,000    260,000,000,000
        United States of America      8,000,000     30,000,000,000
        Iran                          4,000,000     90,000,000,000
        Norway                        3,500,000     11,000,000,000
        Mexico                        3,400,000     50,000,000,000
        China                         3,000,000     25,000,000,000
```

The advantage of using a natural join is that the coding is streamlined. The ON clause is implied, and you do not need to use table aliases to qualify column names that are common to both tables. These two queries return the same results:

```
proc sql;
   select a.W, a.X, Y, Z
   from table1 a left join table2 b
   on a.W=b.W and a.X=b.X
   order by a.W;
```

```
proc sql;
   select W, X, Y, Z
   from table1 natural left join table2
   order by W;
```

If you specify a natural join on tables that do not have at least one column with a common name and type, then the result is a Cartesian product. You can use a WHERE clause to limit the output.

Because the natural join makes certain assumptions about what you want to accomplish, you should know your data thoroughly before using it. You could get unexpected or incorrect results if, for example, you are expecting two tables to have only one column in common when they actually have two. You can use the FEEDBACK option to see exactly how PROC SQL is implementing your query. See "Using PROC SQL Options to Create and Debug Queries" on page 112 for more information about the FEEDBACK option.

A natural join assumes that you want to base the join on equal values of all pairs of common columns. To base the join on inequalities or other comparison operators, use standard inner or outer join syntax.

Using the Coalesce Function in Joins

As you can see from the previous examples, the nonmatching rows in outer joins contain missing values. By using the COALESCE function, you can overlay columns so that only the row from the table that contains data is listed. Recall that COALESCE takes a list of columns as its arguments and returns the first nonmissing value that it encounters.

This example adds the COALESCE function to the previous example to overlay the COUNTRIES.Capital, WORLDCITYCOORDS.City, and COUNTRIES.Name columns. COUNTRIES.Name is supplied as an argument to COALESCE because some islands do not have capitals.

```
proc sql outobs=10;
   title 'Populations and/or Coordinates of World Cities';
   select coalesce(Capital, City,Name)format=$20. 'City',
          coalesce(Name, Country) format=$20. 'Country',
          Population, Latitude, Longitude
      from sql.countries full join sql.worldcitycoords
          on Capital = City and
          Name = Country;
```

Output 3.22   Using COALESCE in Full Outer Join of COUNTRIES and WORLDCITYCOORDS

```
                    Populations and/or Coordinates of World Cities

   City                   Country             Population  Latitude  Longitude
   ----------------------------------------------------------------------------
   Channel Islands        Channel Islands         146436        .         .
   Abadan                 Iran                         .        30        48
   Abu Dhabi              United Arab Emirates    2818628        .         .
   Abuja                  Nigeria                99062003        .         .
   Acapulco               Mexico                       .        17      -100
   Accra                  Ghana                  17395511        5         0
   Adana                  Turkey                       .        37        35
   Addis Ababa            Ethiopia               59291170        9        39
   Adelaide               Australia                    .       -35       138
   Aden                   Yemen                        .        13        45
```

COALESCE can be used in both inner and outer joins. For more information about COALESCE, see "Replacing Missing Values" on page 24.

Comparing DATA Step Match-Merges with PROC SQL Joins

Many SAS users are familiar with using a DATA step to merge data sets. This section compares merges to joins. DATA step match-merges and PROC SQL joins can produce the same results. However, a significant difference between a match-merge and a join is that you do not have to sort the tables before you join them.

When All of the Values Match

When all of the values match in the BY variable and there are no duplicate BY variables, you can use an inner join to produce the same result as a match-merge. To demonstrate this result, here are two tables that have the column Flight in common. The values of Flight are the same in both tables:

```
   FLTSUPER                     FLTDEST


   Flight   Supervisor          Flight   Destination

      145   Kang                   145   Brussels
      150   Miller                 150   Paris
      155   Evanko                 155   Honolulu
```

FLTSUPER and FLTDEST are already sorted by the matching column Flight. A DATA step merge produces Output 3.23.

```
data merged;
   merge FltSuper FltDest;
   by Flight;
run;


proc print data=merged noobs;
   title 'Table MERGED';
run;
```

Output 3.23   Merged Tables When All the Values Match

```
                        Table MERGED

           Flight    Supervisor    Destination

             145      Kang          Brussels
             150      Miller        Paris
             155      Evanko        Honolulu
```

With PROC SQL, presorting the data is not necessary. The following PROC SQL join gives the same result as that shown in Output 3.23.

```
proc sql;
   title 'Table MERGED';
   select s.flight, Supervisor, Destination
      from fltsuper s, fltdest d
      where s.Flight=d.Flight;
```

When Only Some of the Values Match

When only some of the values match in the BY variable, you can use an outer join to produce the same result as a match-merge. To demonstrate this result, here are two tables that have the column Flight in common. The values of Flight are not the same in both tables:

```
FLTSUPER                      FLTDEST

Flight  Supervisor            Flight  Destination

  145   Kang                    145   Brussels
  150   Miller                  150   Paris
  155   Evanko                  165   Seattle
  157   Lei
```

A DATA step merge produces Output 3.24:

```
data merged;
   merge fltsuper fltdest;
   by flight;
run;
proc print data=merged noobs;
   title 'Table MERGED';
run;
```

Output 3.24 Merged Tables When Some of the Values Match

```
                         Table MERGED

            Flight     Supervisor     Destination

             145         Kang           Brussels
             150         Miller         Paris
             155         Evanko
             157         Lei
             165                        Seattle
```

To get the same result with PROC SQL, use an outer join so that the query result will contain the nonmatching rows from the two tables. In addition, use the COALESCE function to overlay the Flight columns from both tables. The following PROC SQL join gives the same result as that shown in Output 3.24:

```
proc sql;
   select coalesce(s.Flight,d.Flight) as Flight, Supervisor, Destination
      from fltsuper s full join fltdest d
          on s.Flight=d.Flight;
```

When the Position of the Values Is Important

When you want to merge two tables and the position of the values is important, you might need to use a DATA step merge. To demonstrate this idea, here are two tables to consider:

```
FLTSUPER                         FLTDEST


Flight   Supervisor              Flight   Destination

  145    Kang                      145    Brussels
  145    Ramirez                   145    Edmonton
  150    Miller                    150    Paris
  150    Picard                    150    Madrid
  155    Evanko                    165    Seattle
  157    Lei
```

For Flight 145, **Kang** matches with **Brussels** and **Ramirez** matches with **Edmonton**. Because the DATA step merges data based on the position of values in BY groups, the values of Supervisor and Destination match appropriately. A DATA step merge produces Output 3.25:

```
data merged;
   merge fltsuper fltdest;
   by flight;
run;
proc print data=merged noobs;
   title 'Table MERGED';
run;
```

Output 3.25   Match-Merge of the FLTSUPER and FLTDEST Tables

```
                         Table MERGED

              Flight    Supervisor    Destination

                145     Kang          Brussels
                145     Ramirez       Edmonton
                150     Miller        Paris
                150     Picard        Madrid
                155     Evanko
                157     Lei
                165                   Seattle
```

PROC SQL does not process joins according to the position of values in BY groups. Instead, PROC SQL processes data only according to the data values. Here is the result of an inner join for FLTSUPER and FLTDEST:

```
proc sql;
   title 'Table JOINED';
   select *
      from fltsuper s, fltdest d
      where s.Flight=d.Flight;
```

Output 3.26   PROC SQL Join of the FLTSUPER and FLTDEST Tables

```
                         Table JOINED

           Flight  Supervisor   Flight  Destination
           -----------------------------------------
              145  Kang            145   Brussels
              145  Kang            145   Edmonton
              145  Ramirez         145   Brussels
              145  Ramirez         145   Edmonton
              150  Miller          150   Paris
              150  Miller          150   Madrid
              150  Picard          150   Paris
              150  Picard          150   Madrid
```

PROC SQL builds the Cartesian product and then lists the rows that meet the WHERE clause condition. The WHERE clause returns two rows for each supervisor, one row for each destination. Because Flight has duplicate values and there is no other matching column, there is no way to associate **Kang** only with **Brussels**, **Ramirez** only with **Edmonton**, and so on.

For more information about DATA step match-merges, see *SAS Language Reference: Dictionary*.

Using Subqueries to Select Data

While a table join combines multiple tables into a new table, a subquery (enclosed in parentheses) selects rows from one table based on values in another table. A subquery, or inner query, is a query-expression that is nested as part of another query-expression.

Depending on the clause that contains it, a subquery can return a single value or multiple values. Subqueries are most often used in the WHERE and the HAVING expressions.

Single-Value Subqueries

A single-value subquery returns a single row and column. It can be used in a WHERE or HAVING clause with a comparison operator. The subquery must return only one value, or else the query fails and an error message is printed to the log.

This query uses a subquery in its WHERE clause to select U.S. states that have a population greater than Belgium. The subquery is evaluated first, and then it returns the population of Belgium to the outer query.

```
proc sql;
   title 'U.S. States with Population Greater than Belgium';
   select Name 'State' , population format=comma10.
      from sql.unitedstates
      where population gt
               (select population from sql.countries
                     where name = "Belgium");
```

Internally, this is what the query looks like after the subquery has executed:

```
proc sql;
   title 'U.S. States with Population Greater than Belgium';
   select Name 'State', population format=comma10.
      from sql.unitedstates
      where population gt 10162614;
```

The outer query lists the states whose populations are greater than the population of Belgium.

Output 3.27 Single-Value Subquery

```
            U.S. States with Population Greater than Belgium

            State                              Population
            ------------------------------------------------
            California                         31,518,948
            Florida                            13,814,408
            Illinois                           11,813,091
            New York                           18,377,334
            Ohio                               11,200,790
            Pennsylvania                       12,167,566
            Texas                              18,209,994
```

Multiple-Value Subqueries

A multiple-value subquery can return more than one value from one column. It is used in a WHERE or HAVING expression that contains IN or a comparison operator that is modified by ANY or ALL. This example displays the populations of oil-producing countries. The subquery first returns all countries that are found in the OILPROD table. The outer query then matches countries in the COUNTRIES table to the results of the subquery.

```
proc sql outobs=5;
   title 'Populations of Major Oil Producing Countries';
   select name 'Country', Population format=comma15.
      from sql.countries
      where Name in
            (select Country from sql.oilprod);
```

Output 3.28   Multiple-Value Subquery Using IN

```
             Populations of Major Oil Producing Countries

          Country                              Population
          ---------------------------------------------------
          Algeria                              28,171,132
          Canada                               28,392,302
          China                             1,202,215,077
          Egypt                                59,912,259
          Indonesia                           202,393,859
```

If you use the NOT IN operator in this query, then the query result will contain all the countries that are *not* contained in the OILPROD table.

```
proc sql outobs=5;
   title 'Populations of NonMajor Oil Producing Countries';
   select name 'Country', Population format=comma15.
      from sql.countries
      where Name not in
            (select Country from sql.oilprod);
```

Output 3.29   Multiple-Value Subquery Using NOT IN

```
            Populations of NonMajor Oil Producing Countries

          Country                              Population
          ---------------------------------------------------
          Afghanistan                          17,070,323
          Albania                               3,407,400
          Andorra                                  64,634
          Angola                                9,901,050
          Antigua and Barbuda                      65,644
```

Correlated Subqueries

The previous subqueries have been simple subqueries that are self-contained and that execute independently of the outer query. A *correlated* subquery requires a value or values to be passed to it by the outer query. After the subquery runs, it passes the results back to the outer query. Correlated subqueries can return single or multiple values.

This example selects all major oil reserves of countries on the continent of Africa.

```
proc sql;
   title 'Oil Reserves of Countries in Africa';
   select * from sql.oilrsrvs o
     where 'Africa' =
                (select Continent from sql.countries c
             where c.Name = o.Country);
```

The outer query selects the first row from the OILRSRVS table and then passes the value of the Country column, **Algeria**, to the subquery. At this point, the subquery internally looks like this:

```
(select Continent from sql.countries c
        where c.Name = 'Algeria');
```

The subquery selects that country from the COUNTRIES table. The subquery then passes the country's continent back to the WHERE clause in the outer query. If the continent is Africa, then the country is selected and displayed. The outer query then selects each subsequent row from the OILRSRVS table and passes the individual values of Country to the subquery. The subquery returns the appropriate values of Continent to the outer query for comparison in its WHERE clause.

Note that the WHERE clause uses an = (equal) operator. You can use an = if the subquery returns only a single value. However, if the subquery returns multiple values, then you must use IN or a comparison operator with ANY or ALL. For detailed information about the operators that are available for use with subqueries, see the section about the SQL procedure in the *Base SAS Procedures Guide*.

Output 3.30   *Correlated Subquery*

```
                Oil Reserves of Countries in Africa

         Country                              Barrels
         -------------------------------------------------
         Algeria                        9,200,000,000
         Egypt                          4,000,000,000
         Gabon                          1,000,000,000
         Libya                         30,000,000,000
         Nigeria                       16,000,000,000
```

Testing for the Existence of a Group of Values

The EXISTS condition tests for the existence of a set of values. An EXISTS condition is true if any rows are produced by the subquery, and it is false if no rows are produced. Conversely, the NOT EXISTS condition is true when a subquery produces an empty table.

This example produces the same result as Output 3.30. EXISTS checks for the existence of countries that have oil reserves on the continent of Africa. Note that the WHERE clause in the subquery now contains the condition **Continent = 'Africa'** that was in the outer query in the previous example.

```
proc sql;
   title 'Oil Reserves of Countries in Africa';
   select * from sql.oilrsrvs o
     where exists
```

```
            (select Continent from sql.countries c
        where o.Country = c.Name and
              Continent = 'Africa');
```

Output 3.31 Testing for the Existence of a Group of Values

```
                    Oil Reserves of Countries in Africa

            Country                                 Barrels
            ---------------------------------------------------
            Algeria                           9,200,000,000
            Egypt                             4,000,000,000
            Gabon                             1,000,000,000
            Libya                            30,000,000,000
            Nigeria                          16,000,000,000
```

Multiple Levels of Subquery Nesting

Subqueries can be nested so that the innermost subquery returns a value or values to be used by the next outer query. Then, that subquery's value or values are used by the next outer query, and so on. Evaluation always begins with the innermost subquery and works outward.

This example lists cities in Africa that are in countries with major oil reserves.

❶ The innermost query is evaluated first. It returns countries that are located on the continent of Africa.

❷ The outer subquery is evaluated. It returns a subset of African countries that have major oil reserves by comparing the list of countries that was returned by the inner subquery against the countries in OILRSRVS.

❸ Finally, the WHERE clause in the outer query lists the coordinates of the cities that exist in the WORLDCITYCOORDS table whose countries match the results of the outer subquery.

```
proc sql;
    title 'Coordinates of African Cities with Major Oil Reserves';
    select * from sql.worldcitycoords
   ❸ where country in
          ❷ (select Country from sql.oilrsrvs o
                where o.Country in =
                       ❶ (select Name from sql.countries c
                       where c.Continent='Africa'));
```

Output 3.32 Multiple Levels of Subquery Nesting

```
                   Coordinates of African Cities with Major Oil Reserves

        City                        Country                    Latitude  Longitude
        -----------------------------------------------------------------------
        Algiers                     Algeria                        37          3
        Cairo                       Egypt                          30         31
        Benghazi                    Libya                          33         21
        Lagos                       Nigeria                         6          3
```

Combining a Join with a Subquery

You can combine joins and subqueries in a single query. Suppose that you want to find the city nearest to each city in the USCITYCOORDS table. The query must first select a city A, compute the distance from city A to every other city, and finally select the city with the minimum distance from city A. This can be done by joining the USCITYCOORDS table to itself (self-join) and then determining the closest distance between cities by using another self-join in a subquery.

This is the formula to determine the distance between coordinates:

```
SQRT(((Latitude2-Latitude1)**2) + ((Longitude2-Longitude1)**2))
```

Although the results of this formula are not exactly accurate because of the distortions caused by the curvature of the earth, they are accurate enough for this example to determine whether one city is closer than another.

```
proc sql outobs=10;
   title 'Neighboring Cities';
   select a.City format=$10., a.State,
          a.Latitude 'Lat', a.Longitude 'Long',
          b.City format=$10., b.State,
          b.Latitude 'Lat', b.Longitude 'Long',
          sqrt(((b.latitude-a.latitude)**2) +
             ((b.longitude-a.longitude)**2)) as dist format=6.1
      from sql.uscitycoords a, sql.uscitycoords b
      where a.city ne b.city and
            calculated dist =
            (select min(sqrt(((d.latitude-c.latitude)**2) +
                          ((d.longitude-c.longitude)**2)))
                from sql.uscitycoords c, sql.uscitycoords d
                where c.city = a.city and
                      c.state = a.state and
                      d.city ne c.city)
            order by a.city;
```

Output 3.33   Combining a Join with a Subquery

```
                          Neighboring Cities

City          State     Lat     Long  City          State      Lat     Long   dist
------------------------------------------------------------------------------------
Albany        NY         43      -74  Hartford      CT          42      -73    1.4
Albuquerqu    NM         36     -106  Santa Fe      NM          36     -106    0.0
Amarillo      TX         35     -102  Carlsbad      NM          32     -104    3.6
Anchorage     AK         61     -150  Nome          AK          64     -165   15.3
Annapolis     MD         39      -77  Washington    DC          39      -77    0.0
Atlanta       GA         34      -84  Knoxville     TN          36      -84    2.0
Augusta       ME         44      -70  Portland      ME          44      -70    0.0
Austin        TX         30      -98  San Antoni    TX          29      -98    1.0
Baker         OR         45     -118  Lewiston      ID          46     -117    1.4
Baltimore     MD         39      -76  Dover         DE          39      -76    0.0
```

The outer query joins the table to itself and determines the distance between the first city A1 in table A and city B2 (the first city that is not equal to city A1) in Table B. PROC SQL then runs the subquery. The subquery does another self-join and calculates the minimum distance between city A1 and all other cities in the table other than city A1. The outer query tests to see whether the distance between cities A1 and B2 is equal to the minimum distance that was calculated by the subquery. If they are equal, then a row that contains cities A1 and B2 with their coordinates and distance is written.

When to Use Joins and Subqueries

Use a join or a subquery any time that you reference information from multiple tables. Joins and subqueries are often used together in the same query. In many cases, you can solve a data retrieval problem by using a join, a subquery, or both. Here are some guidelines for using joins and queries.

- □ If your report needs data that is from more than one table, then you must perform a join. Whenever multiple tables (or views) are listed in the FROM clause, those tables become joined.

- □ If you need to combine related information from different rows within a table, then you can join the table with itself.

- □ Use subqueries when the result that you want requires more than one query and each subquery provides a subset of the table involved in the query.

- □ If a membership question is asked, then a subquery is usually used. If the query requires a NOT EXISTS condition, then you must use a subquery because NOT EXISTS operates only in a subquery; the same principle holds true for the EXISTS condition.

- □ Many queries can be formulated as joins or subqueries. Although the PROC SQL query optimizer changes some subqueries to joins, a join is generally more efficient to process.

Combining Queries with Set Operators

Working with Two or More Query Results

PROC SQL can combine the results of two or more queries in various ways by using the following set operators:

UNION   produces all unique rows from both queries.

EXCEPT   produces rows that are part of the first query only.

INTERSECT   produces rows that are common to both query results.

OUTER UNION   concatenates the query results.

The operator is used between the two queries, for example:

```
select columns from table
set-operator
select columns from table;
```

Place a semicolon after the last SELECT statement only. Set operators combine columns from two queries based on their position in the referenced tables without regard to the individual column names. Columns in the same relative position in the two queries must have the same data types. The column names of the tables in the first query become the column names of the output table. For information about using set operators with more than two query results, see the section about the SQL procedure in the *Base SAS Procedures Guide*. The following optional keywords give you more control over set operations:

ALL
   does not suppress duplicate rows. When the keyword ALL is specified, PROC SQL does not make a second pass through the data to eliminate duplicate rows. Thus, using ALL is more efficient than not using it. ALL is not necessary with the OUTER UNION operator.

CORRESPONDING (CORR)
   overlays columns that have the same name in both tables. When used with EXCEPT, INTERSECT, and UNION, CORR suppresses columns that are not in both tables.

Each set operator is described and used in an example based on the following two tables.

Output 3.34 Tables Used in Set Operation Examples

```
                              Table A

                              x   y
                          ------------------
                              1   one
                              2   two
                              2   two
                              3   three
```

```
                              Table B

                            x   z
                        ------------------
                            1   one
                            2   two
                            4   four
```

Whereas join operations combine tables horizontally, set operations combine tables vertically. Therefore, the set diagrams that are included in each section are displayed vertically.

Producing Unique Rows from Both Queries (UNION)

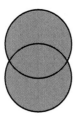

The UNION operator combines two query results. It produces all the unique rows that result from both queries; that is, it returns a row if it occurs in the first table, the second, or both. UNION does not return duplicate rows. If a row occurs more than once, then only one occurrence is returned.

```
proc sql;
    title 'A UNION B';
    select * from sql.a
    union
    select * from sql.b;
```

Output 3.35   Producing Unique Rows from Both Queries (UNION)

```
                            A UNION B

                          x   y
                      ------------------
                          1   one
                          2   two
                          3   three
                          4   four
```

You can use the ALL keyword to request that duplicate rows remain in the output.

```
proc sql;
    title 'A UNION ALL B';
    select * from sql.a
    union all
    select * from sql.b;
```

Output 3.36 Producing Rows from Both Queries (UNION ALL)

```
                              A UNION ALL B

                             x   y
                         ------------------
                             1   one
                             2   two
                             2   two
                             3   three
                             1   one
                             2   two
                             4   four
```

Producing Rows That Are in Only the First Query Result (EXCEPT)

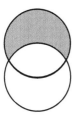

The EXCEPT operator returns rows that result from the first query but not from the second query. In this example, the row that contains the values **3** and **three** exists in the first query (table A) only and is returned by EXCEPT.

```
proc sql;
   title 'A EXCEPT B';
   select * from sql.a
   except
   select * from sql.b;
```

Output 3.37 Producing Rows That Are in Only the First Query Result (EXCEPT)

```
                              A EXCEPT B

                             x   y
                         ------------------
                             3   three
```

Note that the duplicated row in Table A containing the values **2** and **two** does not appear in the output. EXCEPT does not return duplicate rows that are unmatched by rows in the second query. Adding ALL keeps any duplicate rows that do not occur in the second query.

```
proc sql;
   title 'A EXCEPT ALL B';
```

```
select * from sql.a
except all
select * from sql.b;
```

Output 3.38   Producing Rows That Are in Only the First Query Result (EXCEPT ALL)

```
                              A EXCEPT ALL B

                                 x   y
                        ------------------
                                 2   two
                                 3   three
```

Producing Rows That Belong to Both Query Results (INTERSECT)

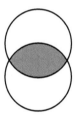

The INTERSECT operator returns rows from the first query that also occur in the second.

```
proc sql;
    title 'A INTERSECT B';
    select * from sql.a
    intersect
    select * from sql.b;
```

Output 3.39   Producing Rows That Belong to Both Query Results (INTERSECT)

```
                              A INTERSECT B

                                 x   y
                        -------------------
                                 1   one
                                 2   two
```

The output of an INTERSECT ALL operation contains the rows produced by the first query that are matched one-to-one with a row produced by the second query. In this example, the output of INTERSECT ALL is the same as INTERSECT.

Concatenating Query Results (OUTER UNION)

The OUTER UNION operator concatenates the results of the queries. This example concatenates tables A and B.

```
proc sql;
   title 'A OUTER UNION B';
   select * from sql.a
   outer union
   select * from sql.b;
```

Output 3.40   Concatenating the Query Results (OUTER UNION)

```
                            A OUTER UNION B

                   x   y                   x   z
                ----------------------------------------
                   1   one                 .
                   2   two                 .
                   2   two                 .
                   3   three               .
                   .                       1   one
                   .                       2   two
                   .                       4   four
```

Notice that OUTER UNION does not overlay columns from the two tables. To overlay columns in the same position, use the CORRESPONDING keyword.

```
proc sql;
   title 'A OUTER UNION CORR B';
   select * from sql.a
   outer union corr
   select * from sql.b;
```

Output 3.41 Concatenating the Query Results (OUTER UNION CORR)

```
                    A OUTER UNION CORR B

                  x   y            z
          ---------------------------
                  1   one
                  2   two
                  2   two
                  3   three
                  1                one
                  2                two
                  4                four
```

Producing Rows from the First Query or the Second Query

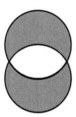

There is no keyword in PROC SQL that returns unique rows from the first and second table, but not rows that occur in both. Here is one way you can simulate this operation:

```
(query1 except query2)
union
(query2 except query1)
```

This example shows how to use this operation.

```
proc sql;
   title 'A EXCLUSIVE UNION B';
   (select * from sql.a
        except
        select * from sql.b)
   union
   (select * from sql.b
        except
        select * from sql.a);
```

Output 3.42 Producing Rows from the First Query or the Second Query

```
                    A EXCLUSIVE UNION B

                       x   y
               ------------------
                       3   three
                       4   four
```

The first EXCEPT returns one unique row from the first table (table A) only. The second EXCEPT returns one unique row from the second table (table B) only. The middle UNION combines the two results. Thus, this query returns the row from the first table that is not in the second table, as well as the row from the second table that is not in the first table.

CHAPTER

4

Creating and Updating Tables and Views

Introduction　**90**
Creating Tables　**90**
　　Creating Tables from Column Definitions　**90**
　　Creating Tables from a Query Result　**91**
　　Creating Tables Like an Existing Table　**92**
　　Copying an Existing Table　**93**
　　Using Data Set Options　**93**
Inserting Rows into Tables　**93**
　　Inserting Rows with the SET Clause　**93**
　　Inserting Rows with the VALUES Clause　**94**
　　Inserting Rows with a Query　**95**
Updating Data Values in a Table　**96**
　　Updating All Rows in a Column with the Same Expression　**96**
　　Updating Rows in a Column with Different Expressions　**97**
　　Handling Update Errors　**98**
Deleting Rows　**98**
Altering Columns　**99**
　　Adding a Column　**99**
　　Modifying a Column　**100**
　　Deleting a Column　**101**
Creating an Index　**102**
　　Using PROC SQL to Create Indexes　**102**
　　Tips for Creating Indexes　**102**
　　Deleting Indexes　**103**
Deleting a Table　**103**
Using SQL Procedure Tables in SAS Software　**103**
Creating and Using Integrity Constraints in a Table　**103**
Creating and Using PROC SQL Views　**106**
　　Creating Views　**106**
　　Describing a View　**107**
　　Updating a View　**107**
　　Embedding a LIBNAME in a View　**107**
　　Deleting a View　**108**
　　Specifying In-Line Views　**108**
　　Tips for Using SQL Procedure Views　**109**
　　Using SQL Procedure Views in SAS Software　**110**

Introduction

This chapter shows you how to

- □ create a table
- □ update tables
- □ alter existing tables
- □ delete a table
- □ create indexes
- □ use integrity constraints in table creation
- □ create views.

Creating Tables

The CREATE TABLE statement enables you to create tables without rows from column definitions or to create tables from a query result. You can also use CREATE TABLE to copy an existing table.

Creating Tables from Column Definitions

You can create a new table without rows by using the CREATE TABLE statement to define the columns and their attributes. You can specify a column's name, type, length, informat, format, and label.

The following CREATE TABLE statement creates the NEWSTATES table:

```
proc sql;
   create table sql.newstates
          (state char(2),           /* 2--character column for          */
                                     /* state abbreviation               */

          date num                   /* column for date of entry into the US */
              informat=date9.        /* with an informat                 */
              format=date9.,         /* and format of DATE9.             */

          population num);           /* column for population            */
```

The table NEWSTATES has three columns and 0 rows. The char(2) modifier is used to change the length for State.

Use the DESCRIBE TABLE statement to verify that the table exists and to see the column attributes. The following DESCRIBE TABLE statement writes a CREATE TABLE statement to the SAS log:

```
proc sql;
   describe table sql.newstates;
```

Output 4.1   Table Created from Column Definitions

```
1  proc sql;
2     describe table sql.newstates;
NOTE: SQL table SQL.NEWSTATES was created like:

create table SQL.NEWSTATES( bufsize=8192 )
  (
   state char(2),
   date num format=DATE9. informat=DATE9.,
   population num
  );
```

DESCRIBE TABLE writes a CREATE TABLE statement to the SAS log even if you did not create the table with the CREATE TABLE statement. You can also use the CONTENTS statement in the DATASETS procedure to get a description of NEWSTATES.

Creating Tables from a Query Result

To create a PROC SQL table from a query result, use a CREATE TABLE statement, and place it before the SELECT statement. When a table is created this way, its data is derived from the table or view that is referenced in the query's FROM clause. The new table's column names are as specified in the query's SELECT clause list. The column attributes (the type, length, informat, and format) are the same as those of the selected source columns.

The following CREATE TABLE statement creates the DENSITIES table from the COUNTRIES table. The newly created table is not displayed in SAS output unless you query the table. Note the use of the OUTOBS option, which limits the size of the DENSITIES table to 10 rows.

```
proc sql outobs=10;
   title 'Densities of Countries';
   create table sql.densities as
      select Name 'Country' format $15.,
             Population format=comma10.0,
             Area as SquareMiles,
             Population/Area format=6.2 as Density
         from sql.countries;

   select * from sql.densities;
```

Output 4.2   Table Created from a Query Result

```
                     Densities of Countries

        Country          Population  SquareMiles  Density
        ------------------------------------------------
        Afghanistan      17,070,323       251825    67.79
        Albania           3,407,400        11100   306.97
        Algeria          28,171,132       919595    30.63
        Andorra              64,634          200   323.17
        Angola            9,901,050       481300    20.57
        Antigua and Bar      65,644          171   383.88
        Argentina        34,248,705      1073518    31.90
        Armenia           3,556,864        11500   309.29
        Australia        18,255,944      2966200     6.15
        Austria           8,033,746        32400   247.96
```

The following DESCRIBE TABLE statement writes a CREATE TABLE statement to the SAS log:

```
proc sql;
   describe table sql.densities;
```

Output 4.3   SAS Log for DESCRIBE TABLE Statement for DENSITIES

```
NOTE: SQL table SQL.DENSITIES was created like:

create table SQL.DENSITIES( bufsize=8192 )
   (
   Name char(35) format=$15. informat=$35. label='Country',
   Population num format=COMMA10. informat=BEST8. label='Population',
   SquareMiles num format=BEST8. informat=BEST8. label='SquareMiles',
   Density num format=6.2
   );
```

In this form of the CREATE TABLE statement, assigning an alias to a column renames the column, while assigning a label does not. In this example, the Area column has been renamed to SquareMiles, and the calculated column has been named Densities. However, the Name column retains its name, and its display label is **Country**.

Creating Tables Like an Existing Table

To create an empty table that has the same columns and attributes as an existing table or view, use the LIKE clause in the CREATE TABLE statement. In the following example, the CREATE TABLE statement creates the NEWCOUNTRIES table with six columns and 0 rows and with the same column attributes as those in COUNTRIES. The DESCRIBE TABLE statement writes a CREATE TABLE statement to the SAS log:

```
proc sql;
   create table sql.newcountries
      like sql.countries;

   describe table sql.newcountries;
```

Output 4.4 SAS Log for DESCRIBE TABLE Statement for NEWCOUNTRIES

```
NOTE: SQL table SQL.NEWCOUNTRIES was created like:

create table SQL.NEWCOUNTRIES( bufsize=16384 )
  (
   Name char(35) format=$35. informat=$35.,
   Capital char(35) format=$35. informat=$35. label='Capital',
   Population num format=BEST8. informat=BEST8. label='Population',
   Area num format=BEST8. informat=BEST8.,
   Continent char(35) format=$35. informat=$35. label='Continent',
   UNDate num format=YEAR4.
  );
```

Copying an Existing Table

A quick way to copy a table using PROC SQL is to use the CREATE TABLE statement with a query that returns an entire table. This example creates COUNTRIES1, which contains a copy of all the columns and rows that are in COUNTRIES:

```
create table countries1 as
   select * from sql.countries;
```

Using Data Set Options

You can use SAS data set options in the CREATE TABLE statement. The following CREATE TABLE statement creates COUNTRIES2 from COUNTRIES. The DROP= option deletes the UNDate column, and UNDate does not become part of COUNTRIES2:

```
create table countries2 as
   select * from sql.countries(drop=UNDate);
```

Inserting Rows into Tables

Use the INSERT statement to insert data values into tables. The INSERT statement first adds a new row to an existing table, and then inserts the values that you specify into the row. You specify values by using a SET clause or VALUES clause. You can also insert the rows resulting from a query.

Under most conditions, you can insert data into tables through PROC SQL and SAS/ACCESS views. See "Updating a View" on page 107.

Inserting Rows with the SET Clause

With the SET clause, you assign values to columns by name. The columns can appear in any order in the SET clause. The following INSERT statement uses multiple SET clauses to add two rows to NEWCOUNTRIES:

```
proc sql;
   insert into sql.newcountries
```

```
      set name='Bangladesh',
          capital='Dhaka',
          population=126391060
      set name='Japan',
          capital='Tokyo',
          population=126352003;

  title "World's Largest Countries";
  select name format=$20.,
         capital format=$15.,
         population format=comma15.0
      from sql.newcountries;
```

Output 4.5   Rows Inserted with the SET Clause

```
                        World's Largest Countries

          Name                Capital           Population
          ------------------------------------------------------
          Brazil              Brasilia             160,310,357
          China               Beijing            1,202,215,077
          India               New Delhi            929,009,120
          Indonesia           Jakarta              202,393,859
          Russia              Moscow               151,089,979
          United States       Washington           263,294,808
          Bangladesh          Dhaka                126,391,060
          Japan               Tokyo                126,352,003
```

Note the following features of SET clauses:

□ As with other SQL clauses, use commas to separate columns. In addition, you must use a semicolon after the last SET clause only.

□ If you omit data for a column, then the value in that column is a missing value.

□ To specify that a value is missing, use a blank in single quotation marks for character values and a period for numeric values.

Inserting Rows with the VALUES Clause

With the VALUES clause, you assign values to a column by position. The following INSERT statement uses multiple VALUES clauses to add rows to NEWCOUNTRIES. Recall that NEWCOUNTRIES has six columns, so it is necessary to specify a value or an appropriate missing value for all six columns. See the results of the DESCRIBE TABLE statement in "Creating Tables Like an Existing Table" on page 92 for information about the columns of NEWCOUNTRIES.

```
  proc sql;
     insert into sql.newcountries
        values ('Pakistan', 'Islamabad', 123060000, ., ' ', .)
        values ('Nigeria', 'Lagos', 99062000, ., ' ', .);
     title "World's Largest Countries";
     select name format=$20.,
            capital format=$15.,
            population format=comma15.0
        from sql.newcountries;
```

Output 4.6 Rows Inserted with the Values Clause

```
                          World's Largest Countries

            Name                  Capital           Population
            --------------------------------------------------
            Brazil                Brasilia            160,310,357
            China                 Beijing           1,202,215,077
            India                 New Delhi           929,009,120
            Indonesia             Jakarta             202,393,859
            Russia                Moscow              151,089,979
            United States         Washington          263,294,808
            Pakistan              Islamabad           123,060,000
            Nigeria               Lagos                99,062,000
```

Note the following features of VALUES clauses:

☐ As with other SQL clauses, use commas to separate columns. In addition, you must use a semicolon after the last VALUES clause only.

☐ If you omit data for a column without indicating a missing value, then you receive an error message and the row is not inserted.

☐ To specify that a value is missing, use a space in single quotation marks for character values and a period for numeric values.

Inserting Rows with a Query

You can insert the rows from a query result into a table. The following query returns rows for large countries (over 130 million in population) from the COUNTRIES table. The INSERT statement adds the data to the empty table NEWCOUNTRIES, which was created earlier in "Creating Tables Like an Existing Table" on page 92:

```
proc sql;
   create table sql.newcountries
      like sql.countries;


proc sql;
   title "World's Largest Countries";
   insert into sql.newcountries
   select * from sql.countries
      where population ge 130000000;

   select name format=$20.,
          capital format=$15.,
          population format=comma15.0
      from sql.newcountries;
```

Output 4.7   Rows Inserted with a Query

```
                         World's Largest Countries

        Name                    Capital              Population
        ----------------------------------------------------------
        Brazil                  Brasilia                160,310,357
        China                   Beijing               1,202,215,077
        India                   New Delhi               929,009,120
        Indonesia               Jakarta                 202,393,859
        Russia                  Moscow                  151,089,979
        United States           Washington              263,294,808
```

If your query does not return data for every column, then you receive an error message, and the row is not inserted. For more information about how PROC SQL handles errors during data insertions, see "Handling Update Errors" on page 98.

Updating Data Values in a Table

You can use the UPDATE statement to modify data values in tables and in the tables that underlie PROC SQL and SAS/ACCESS views. For more information about updating views, see "Updating a View" on page 107. The UPDATE statement updates data in existing columns; it does not create new columns. To add new columns, see "Altering Columns" on page 99 and "Creating New Columns" on page 18. The examples in this section update the original NEWCOUNTRIES table.

Updating All Rows in a Column with the Same Expression

The following UPDATE statement increases all populations in the NEWCOUNTRIES table by five percent:

```
proc sql;
   update sql.newcountries
      set population=population*1.05;
   title "Updated Population Values";
   select name format=$20.,
          capital format=$15.,
          population format=comma15.0
      from sql.newcountries;
```

Output 4.8 Updating a Column for All Rows

```
                      Updated Population Values

        Name                  Capital            Population
        ------------------------------------------------------
        Brazil                Brasilia              168,325,875
        China                 Beijing             1,262,325,831
        India                 New Delhi             975,459,576
        Indonesia             Jakarta               212,513,552
        Russia                Moscow                158,644,478
        United States         Washington            276,459,548
```

Updating Rows in a Column with Different Expressions

If you want to update some, but not all, of a column's values, then use a WHERE expression in the UPDATE statement. You can use multiple UPDATE statements, each with a different expression. However, each UPDATE statement can have only one WHERE clause. The following UPDATE statements result in different population increases for different countries in the NEWCOUNRTRIES table.

```
proc sql;
   update sql.newcountries
      set population=population*1.05
         where name like 'B%';

   update sql.newcountries
      set population=population*1.07
         where name in ('China', 'Russia');

   title "Selectively Updated Population Values";
   select name format=$20.,
          capital format=$15.,
          population format=comma15.0
      from sql.newcountries;
```

Output 4.9 Selectively Updating a Column

```
                 Selectively Updated Population Values

        Name                  Capital            Population
        ------------------------------------------------------
        Brazil                Brasilia              168,325,875
        China                 Beijing             1,286,370,132
        India                 New Delhi             929,009,120
        Indonesia             Jakarta               202,393,859
        Russia                Moscow                161,666,278
        United States         Washington            263,294,808
```

You can accomplish the same result with a CASE expression:

```
update sql.newcountries
   set population=population*
```

```
case when name like 'B%' then 1.05
     when name in ('China', 'Russia') then 1.07
     else 1
end;
```

If the WHEN clause is true, then the corresponding THEN clause returns a value that the SET clause then uses to complete its expression. In this example, when Name starts with the letter *B*, the SET expression becomes **population=population*1.05**.

CAUTION:

Make sure that you specify the ELSE clause. If you omit the ELSE clause, then each row that is not described in one of the WHEN clauses receives a missing value for the column that you are updating. This happens because the CASE expression supplies a missing value to the SET clause, and the Population column is multiplied by a missing value, which produces a missing value. △

Handling Update Errors

While you are updating or inserting rows in a table, you might receive an error message that the update or insert cannot be performed. By using the UNDO_POLICY= option, you can control whether the changes that have already been made will be permanent.

The UNDO _POLICY= option in the PROC SQL and RESET statements determines how PROC SQL handles the rows that have been inserted or updated by the current INSERT or UPDATE statement up to the point of error.

UNDO_POLICY=REQUIRED
    is the default. It undoes all updates or inserts up to the point of error.

UNDO_POLICY=NONE
    does not undo any updates or inserts.

UNDO_POLICY=OPTIONAL
    undoes any updates or inserts that it can undo reliably.

Note: Alternatively, you can set the SQLUNDOPOLICY system option. For more information, see the SQLUNDOPOLICY system option in *SAS Language Reference: Dictionary.* △

Deleting Rows

The DELETE statement deletes one or more rows in a table or in a table that underlies a PROC SQL or SAS/ACCESS view. For more information about deleting rows from views, see "Updating a View" on page 107. The following DELETE statement deletes the names of countries that begin with the letter *R*:

```
proc sql;
   delete
      from sql.newcountries
      where name like 'R%';
```

A note in the SAS log tells you how many rows were deleted.

Output 4.10 SAS Log for DELETE statement

```
NOTE: 1 row was deleted from SQL.NEWCOUNTRIES.
```

Note: For PROC SQL tables, SAS deletes the data in the rows but retains the space in the table. △

CAUTION:
If you use the DELETE statement without a WHERE clause, then all rows are deleted. △

Altering Columns

The ALTER TABLE statement adds, modifies, and deletes columns in existing tables. You can use the ALTER TABLE statement with tables only; it does not work with views. A note appears in the SAS log that describes how you have modified the table.

Adding a Column

The ADD clause adds a new column to an existing table. You must specify the column name and data type. You can also specify a length (LENGTH=), format (FORMAT=), informat (INFORMAT=), and a label (LABEL=). The following ALTER TABLE statement adds the numeric data column Density to the NEWCOUNTRIES table:

```
proc sql;
   alter table sql.newcountries
      add density num label='Population Density' format=6.2;

   title "Population Density Table";
   select name format=$20.,
          capital format=$15.,
          population format=comma15.0,
          density
      from sql.newcountries;
```

Output 4.11 Adding a New Column

```
                         Population Density Table

                                                           Population
         Name                 Capital            Population   Density
         ------------------------------------------------------------
         Brazil               Brasilia          160,310,357       .
         China                Beijing         1,202,215,077       .
         India                New Delhi         929,009,120       .
         Indonesia            Jakarta           202,393,859       .
         Russia               Moscow            151,089,979       .
         United States        Washington        263,294,808       .
```

The new column is added to NEWCOUNTRIES, but it has no data values. The following UPDATE statement changes the missing values for Density from missing to the appropriate population densities for each country:

```
proc sql;
   update sql.newcountries
      set density=population/area;

   title "Population Density Table";
   select name format=$20.,
          capital format=$15.,
          population format=comma15.0,
          density
      from sql.newcountries;
```

Output 4.12 Filling in the New Column's Values

```
                         Population Density Table

                                                             Population
        Name                 Capital              Population    Density
        -------------------------------------------------------------------
        Brazil               Brasilia           160,310,357      48.78
        China                Beijing          1,202,215,077     325.27
        India                New Delhi          929,009,120     759.86
        Indonesia            Jakarta            202,393,859     273.10
        Russia               Moscow             151,089,979      22.92
        United States        Washington         263,294,808      69.52
```

For more information about how to change data values, see "Updating Data Values in a Table" on page 96.

You can accomplish the same update by using an arithmetic expression to create the Population Density column as you recreate the table:

```
proc sql;
   create table sql.newcountries as
   select *, population/area as density
          label='Population Density'
          format=6.2
      from sql.newcountries;
```

See "Calculating Values" on page 19 for another example of creating columns with arithmetic expressions.

Modifying a Column

You can use the MODIFY clause to change the width, informat, format, and label of a column. To change a column's name, use the RENAME= data set option. You cannot change a column's data type by using the MODIFY clause.

The following MODIFY clause permanently changes the format for the Population column:

```
proc sql;
   title "World's Largest Countries";
   alter table sql.newcountries
```

```
     modify population format=comma15.;
select name, population from sql.newcountries;
```

Output 4.13 Modifying a Column Format

```
                        World's Largest Countries

     Name                                         Population
     ---------------------------------------------------------
     Brazil                                      160,310,357
     China                                     1,202,215,077
     India                                       929,009,120
     Indonesia                                   202,393,859
     Russia                                      151,089,979
     United States                               263,294,808
```

You might have to change a column's width (and format) before you can update the column. For example, before you can prefix a long text string to Name, you must change the width and format of Name from 35 to 60. The following statements modify and update the Name column:

```
proc sql;
   title "World's Largest Countries";
   alter table sql.newcountries
      modify name char(60) format=$60.;
   update sql.newcountries
      set name='The United Nations member country is '||name;

   select name from sql.newcountries;
```

Output 4.14 Changing a Column's Width

```
                        World's Largest Countries

     Name
     ---------------------------------------------------------------
     The United Nations member country is Brazil
     The United Nations member country is China
     The United Nations member country is India
     The United Nations member country is Indonesia
     The United Nations member country is Russia
     The United Nations member country is United States
```

Deleting a Column

The DROP clause deletes columns from tables. The following DROP clause deletes UNDate from NEWCOUNTRIES:

```
proc sql;
   alter table sql.newcountries
      drop undate;
```

Creating an Index

An *index* is a file that is associated with a table. The index enables access to rows by index value. Indexes can provide quick access to small subsets of data, and they can enhance table joins. You can create indexes, but you cannot instruct PROC SQL to use an index. PROC SQL determines whether it is efficient to use the index.

Some columns might not be appropriate for an index. In general, create indexes for columns that have many unique values or are columns that you use regularly in joins.

Using PROC SQL to Create Indexes

You can create a simple index, which applies to one column only. The name of a simple index must be the same as the name of the column that it indexes. Specify the column name in parentheses after the table name. The following CREATE INDEX statement creates an index for the Area column in NEWCOUNTRIES:

```
proc sql;
   create index area
      on sql.newcountries(area);
```

You can also create a composite index, which applies to two or more columns. The following CREATE INDEX statement creates the index Places for the Name and Continent columns in NEWCOUNTRIES:

```
proc sql;
   create index places
      on sql.newcountries(name, continent);
```

To ensure that each value of the indexed column (or each combination of values of the columns in a composite index) is unique, use the UNIQUE keyword:

```
proc sql;
   create unique index places
      on sql.newcountries(name, continent);
```

Using the UNIQUE keyword causes SAS to reject any change to a table that would cause more than one row to have the same index value.

Tips for Creating Indexes

- □ The name of the composite index cannot be the same as the name of one of the columns in the table.
- □ If you use two columns to access data regularly, such as a first name column and a last name column from an employee database, then you should create a composite index for the columns.
- □ Keep the number of indexes to a minimum to reduce disk space and update costs.
- □ Use indexes for queries that retrieve a relatively small number of rows (less than 15%).
- □ In general, indexing a small table does not result in a performance gain.
- □ In general, indexing on a column with a small number (less than 6 or 7) of distinct values does not result in a performance gain.

□ You can use the same column in a simple index and in a composite index. However, for tables that have a primary key integrity constraint, do not create more than one index that is based on the same column as the primary key.

Deleting Indexes

To delete an index from a table, use the DROP INDEX statement. The following DROP INDEX statement deletes the index Places from NEWCOUNTRIES:

```
proc sql;
   drop index places from sql.newcountries;
```

Deleting a Table

To delete a PROC SQL table, use the DROP TABLE statement:

```
proc sql;
   drop table sql.newcountries;
```

Using SQL Procedure Tables in SAS Software

Because PROC SQL tables are SAS data files, you can use them as input to a DATA step or to other SAS procedures. For example, the following PROC MEANS step calculates the mean for Area for all countries in COUNTRIES:

```
proc means data=sql.countries mean maxdec=2;
   title "Mean Area for All Countries";
   var area;
run;
```

Output 4.15 Using a PROC SQL Table in PROC MEANS

```
                    Mean Area for All Countries

                       The MEANS Procedure

                    Analysis Variable : Area

                              Mean
                        ------------
                          250249.01
                        ------------
```

Creating and Using Integrity Constraints in a Table

Integrity constraints are rules that you specify to guarantee the accuracy, completeness, or consistency of data in tables. All integrity constraints are enforced when you insert, delete, or alter data values in the columns of a table for which integrity constraints have been defined. Before a constraint is added to a table that contains existing data, all the data is checked to determine that it satisfies the constraints.

You can use *general* integrity constraints to verify that data in a column is

- □ nonmissing
- □ unique
- □ both nonmissing and unique
- □ within a specified set or range of values.

You can also apply *referential* integrity constraints to link the values in a specified column (called a *primary key*) of one table to values of a specified column in another table. When linked to a primary key, a column in the second table is called a *foreign key*.

When you define referential constraints, you can also choose what action occurs when a value in the primary key is updated or deleted.

- □ You can prevent the primary key value from being updated or deleted when matching values exist in the foreign key. This is the default.
- □ You can allow updates and deletions to the primary key values. By default, any affected foreign key values are changed to missing values. However, you can specify the CASCADE option to update foreign key values instead. Currently, the CASCADE option does not apply to deletions.

You can choose separate actions for updates and for deletions.

Note: Integrity constraints cannot be defined for views. △

The following example creates integrity constraints for a table, MYSTATES, and another table, USPOSTAL. The constraints are as follows:

- □ state name must be unique and nonmissing in both tables
- □ population must be greater than 0
- □ continent must be either North America or Oceania.

```
proc sql;
   create table sql.mystates
      (state      char(15),
       population num,
       continent  char(15),

          /* contraint specifications */
       constraint prim_key    primary key(state),
       constraint population   check(population gt 0),
       constraint continent    check(continent in ('North America', 'Oceania')));

   create table sql.uspostal
      (name       char(15),
       code       char(2) not null,          /* constraint specified as   */
                                             /* a column attribute        */

       constraint for_key foreign key(name) /* links NAME to the         */
                  references sql.mystates    /* primary key in MYSTATES    */

                  on delete restrict         /* forbids deletions to STATE */
                                             /* unless there is no         */
                                             /* matching NAME value        */

                  on update set null);       /* allows updates to STATE,    */
```

```
                                        /* changes matching NAME    */
                                        /* values to missing        */
```

   The DESCRIBE TABLE statement displays the integrity constraints in the SAS log as part of the table description. The DESCRIBE TABLE CONSTRAINTS statement writes only the constraint specifications to the SAS log.

```
proc sql;
   describe table sql.mystates;
   describe table constraints sql.uspostal;
```

Output 4.16 SAS Log Showing Integrity Constraints

```
NOTE: SQL table SQL.MYSTATES was created like:

create table SQL.MYSTATES( bufsize=8192 )
  (
   state char(15),
   population num,
   continent char(15)
  );
create unique index state on SQL.MYSTATES(state);



              -----Alphabetic List of Integrity Constraints-----

   Integrity                      Where                    On      On
 # Constraint Type    Variables Clause         Reference Delete  Update
------------------------------------------------------------------------------
-49 continent  Check                 continent in
                                     ('North
                                     America',
                                     'Oceania')
-48 population Check                 population>0
-47 prim_key   Primary Key state
   for_key    Referential name                 SQL.       Restrict Set Null
                                               USPOSTAL
NOTE: SQL table SQL.USPOSTAL ( bufsize=8192 ) has the following integrity
      constraints:



              -----Alphabetic List of Integrity Constraints-----

   Integrity                                    On      On
 # Constraint  Type         Variables Reference  Delete  Update
------------------------------------------------------------------------------
 1  _NM0001_   Not Null     code
 2  for_key    Foreign Key  name      SQL.MYSTATES  Restrict  Set Null
```

   Integrity constraints cannot be used in views. For more information about integrity constraints, see *SAS Language Reference: Concepts*.

Creating and Using PROC SQL Views

A PROC SQL view contains a stored query that is executed when you use the view in a SAS procedure or DATA step. Views are useful because they

☐ often save space, because a view is frequently quite small compared with the data that it accesses.

☐ prevent users from continually submitting queries to omit unwanted columns or rows.

☐ shield sensitive or confidential columns from users while enabling the same users to view other columns in the same table.

☐ ensure that input data sets are always current, because data is derived from tables at execution time.

☐ hide complex joins or queries from users.

Creating Views

To create a PROC SQL view, use the CREATE VIEW statement, as shown in the following example:

```
proc sql;
   title 'Current Population Information for Continents';
   create view sql.newcontinents as
   select continent,
          sum(population) as totpop  format=comma15. label='Total Population',
          sum(area) as totarea format=comma15. label='Total Area'
      from sql.countries
      group by continent;

   select * from sql.newcontinents;
```

Output 4.17 An SQL Procedure View

```
                  Current Population Information for Continents

                                            Total
           Continent                     Population      Total Area
           -------------------------------------------------------------

                                            384,772         876,800
           Africa                       710,529,592      11,299,595
           Asia                       3,381,858,879      12,198,325
           Australia                     18,255,944       2,966,200
           Central America and Caribbean 66,815,930         291,463
           Europe                       813,335,288       9,167,084
           North America                384,801,818       8,393,092
           Oceania                        5,342,368         129,600
           South America                317,568,801       6,885,418
```

Note: In this example, each column has a name. If you are planning to use a view in a procedure that requires variable names, then you must supply column aliases that you can reference as variable names in other procedures. For more information, see "Using SQL Procedure Views in SAS Software" on page 110. △

Describing a View

The DESCRIBE VIEW statement writes a description of the PROC SQL view to the SAS log. The following SAS log describes the view NEWCONTINENTS, which is created in "Creating Views" on page 106:

```
proc sql;
   describe view sql.newcontinents;
```

Output 4.18 SAS Log from DESCRIBE VIEW Statement

```
NOTE: SQL view SQL.NEWCONTINENTS is defined as:

      select continent, SUM(population) as totpop label='Total Population'
format=COMMA15.0, SUM(area) as totarea label='Total Area' format=COMMA15.0
         from SQL.COUNTRIES
      group by continent;
```

Updating a View

You can update data through a PROC SQL and SAS/ACCESS view with the INSERT, DELETE, and UPDATE statements, under the following conditions.

☐ You can update only a single table through a view. The underlying table cannot be joined to another table or linked to another table with a set operator. The view cannot contain a subquery.

☐ If the view accesses a DBMS table, then you must have been granted the appropriate authorization by the external database management system (for example, ORACLE). You must have installed the SAS/ACCESS software for your DBMS. See the SAS/ACCESS documentation for your DBMS for more information about SAS/ACCESS views.

☐ You can update a column in a view by using the column's alias, but you cannot update a derived column, that is, a column that is produced by an expression. In the following example, you can update SquareMiles, but not Density:

```
proc sql;
   create view mycountries as
      select Name,
             area as SquareMiles,
             population/area as Density
         from sql.countries;
```

☐ You can update a view that contains a WHERE clause. The WHERE clause can be in the UPDATE clause or in the view. You cannot update a view that contains any other clause, such as ORDER BY, HAVING, and so on.

Embedding a LIBNAME in a View

You can embed a SAS LIBNAME statement or a SAS/ACCESS LIBNAME statement in a view by using the USING LIBNAME clause. When PROC SQL executes the view, the stored query assigns the libref. For SAS/ACCESS librefs, PROC SQL establishes a connection to a DBMS. The scope of the libref is local to the view and does not conflict with any identically named librefs in the SAS session. When the query finishes, the libref is disassociated. The connection to the DBMS is terminated and all data in the library becomes unavailable.

The advantage of embedded librefs is that you can store engine-host options and DBMS connection information, such as passwords, in the view. That, in turn, means that you do not have to remember and reenter that information when you want to use the libref.

Note: The USING LIBNAME clause must be the last clause in the SELECT statement. Multiple clauses can be specified, separated by commas. △

In the following example, the libref OILINFO is assigned and a connection is made to an ORACLE database:

```
proc sql;
   create view sql.view1 as
      select *
         from oilinfo.reserves as newreserves
         using libname oilinfo oracle
            user=username
            pass=password
            path='dbms-path';
```

For more information about the SAS/ACCESS LIBNAME statement, see the SAS/ACCESS documentation for your DBMS.

The following example embeds a SAS LIBNAME statement in a view:

```
proc sql;
   create view sql.view2 as
      select *
         from oil.reserves
         using libname oil 'SAS-data-library';
```

Deleting a View

To delete a view, use the DROP VIEW statement:

```
proc sql;
   drop view sql.newcontinents;
```

Specifying In-Line Views

In some cases, you might want to use a query in a FROM clause instead of a table or view. You could create a view and refer to it in your FROM clause, but that process involves two steps. To save the extra step, specify the view in-line, enclosed in parentheses, in the FROM clause.

An *in-line view* is a query that appears in the FROM clause. An in-line view produces a table internally that the outer query uses to select data. Unlike views that are created with the CREATE VIEW statement, in-line views are not assigned names and cannot be referenced in other queries or SAS procedures as if they were tables. An in-line view can be referenced only in the query in which it is defined.

In the following query, the populations of all Caribbean and Central American countries are summed in an in-line query. The WHERE clause compares the sum with the populations of individual countries. Only countries that have a population greater than the sum of Caribbean and Central American populations are displayed.

```
proc sql;
   title 'Countries With Population GT Caribbean Countries';
   select w.Name, w.Population format=comma15., c.TotCarib
      from (select sum(population) as TotCarib format=comma15.
               from sql.countries
         where continent = 'Central America and Caribbean') as c,
         sql.countries as w
      where w.population gt c.TotCarib;
```

Output 4.19 Using an In-Line View

```
                    Countries With Population GT Caribbean Countries

         Name                                    Population        TotCarib
         -------------------------------------------------------------------
         Bangladesh                             126,387,850      66,815,930
         Brazil                                 160,310,357      66,815,930
         China                                1,202,215,077      66,815,930
         Germany                                 81,890,690      66,815,930
         India                                  929,009,120      66,815,930
         Indonesia                              202,393,859      66,815,930
         Japan                                  126,345,434      66,815,930
         Mexico                                  93,114,708      66,815,930
         Nigeria                                 99,062,003      66,815,930
         Pakistan                               123,062,252      66,815,930
         Philippines                             70,500,039      66,815,930
         Russia                                 151,089,979      66,815,930
         United States                          263,294,808      66,815,930
         Vietnam                                 73,827,657      66,815,930
```

Tips for Using SQL Procedure Views

☐ Avoid using an ORDER BY clause in a view. If you specify an ORDER BY clause, then the data must be sorted each time that the view is referenced.

☐ If data is used many times in one program or in multiple programs, then it is more efficient to create a table rather than a view. If a view is referenced often in one program, then the data must be accessed at each reference.

☐ If the view resides in the same SAS library as the contributing table or tables, then specify a one-level name in the FROM clause. The default for the libref for the FROM clause's table or tables is the libref of the library that contains the view. This prevents you from having to change the view if you assign a different libref to the SAS library that contains the view and its contributing table or tables. This tip is used in the view that is described in "Creating Views" on page 106.

☐ Avoid creating views that are based on tables whose structure might change. A view is no longer valid when it references a nonexistent column.

☐ When you process PROC SQL views between a client and a server, getting the correct results depends on the compatibility between the client and server architecture. For more information, see "Accessing a SAS View" in the *SAS/CONNECT User's Guide*.

Using SQL Procedure Views in SAS Software

You can use PROC SQL views as input to a DATA step or to other SAS procedures. The syntax for using a PROC SQL view in SAS is the same as that for a PROC SQL table. For an example, see "Using SQL Procedure Tables in SAS Software" on page 103.

CHAPTER

5

Programming with the SQL Procedure

Introduction   **112**
Using PROC SQL Options to Create and Debug Queries   **112**
　Restricting Row Processing with the INOBS= and OUTOBS= Options   **112**
　Limiting Iterations with the LOOPS= Option   **113**
　Checking Syntax with the NOEXEC Option and the VALIDATE Statement   **113**
　*Expanding SELECT * with the FEEDBACK Option*   **113**
　Timing PROC SQL with the STIMER Option   **114**
　Resetting PROC SQL Options with the RESET Statement   **115**
Improving Query Performance   **116**
　Using Indexes to Improve Performance   **116**
　Using the Keyword ALL in Set Operations   **117**
　Omitting the ORDER BY Clause When Creating Tables and Views   **117**
　Using In-Line Views versus Temporary Tables   **117**
　Comparing Subqueries with Joins   **117**
　Using WHERE Expressions with Joins   **117**
　Optimizing the PUT Function   **118**
　　Reducing the PUT Function   **118**
　　Deploying the PUT Function and SAS Formats inside Teradata   **119**
　Replacing References to the DATE, TIME, DATETIME, and TODAY Functions   **119**
　Disabling the Remerging of Data When Using Summary Functions   **120**
Accessing SAS System Information by Using DICTIONARY Tables   **120**
　What Are Dictionary Tables?   **120**
　Retrieving Information about DICTIONARY Tables and SASHELP Views   **122**
　Using DICTIONARY.TABLES   **124**
　Using DICTIONARY.COLUMNS   **125**
　DICTIONARY Tables and Performance   **126**
Using SAS Data Set Options with PROC SQL   **127**
Using PROC SQL with the SAS Macro Facility   **128**
　Creating Macro Variables in PROC SQL   **128**
　　Creating Macro Variables from the First Row of a Query Result   **128**
　　Creating a Macro Variable from the Result of an Aggregate Function   **129**
　　Creating Multiple Macro Variables   **129**
　Concatenating Values in Macro Variables   **130**
　Defining Macros to Create Tables   **131**
　Using the PROC SQL Automatic Macro Variables   **133**
Formatting PROC SQL Output by Using the REPORT Procedure   **136**
Accessing a DBMS with SAS/ACCESS Software   **137**
　Connecting to a DBMS by Using the LIBNAME Statement   **138**
　　Querying a DBMS Table   **138**
　　Creating a PROC SQL View of a DBMS Table   **139**
　Connecting to a DBMS by Using the SQL Procedure Pass-Through Facility   **140**

What Is the Pass-Through Facility?   **140**
Return Codes   **141**
Pass-Through Example   **141**
Updating PROC SQL and SAS/ACCESS Views   **142**
Using the Output Delivery System with PROC SQL   **142**

Introduction

This section shows you how to do the following:

□ use PROC SQL options to create and debug queries

□ improve query performance

□ explain dictionary tables and how they are useful in gathering information about the elements of SAS

□ use PROC SQL with the SAS macro facility

□ use PROC SQL with the REPORT procedure

□ access DBMSs by using SAS/ACCESS software

□ format PROC SQL output by using the SAS Output Delivery System (ODS).

Using PROC SQL Options to Create and Debug Queries

PROC SQL supports options that can give you greater control over PROC SQL while you are developing a query:

□ The INOBS=, OUTOBS=, and LOOPS= options reduce query execution time by limiting the number of rows and the number of iterations that PROC SQL processes.

□ The EXEC and VALIDATE statements enable you to quickly check the syntax of a query.

□ The FEEDBACK option displays the columns that are represented by a SELECT * statement.

□ The PROC SQL STIMER option records and displays query execution time.

You can set an option initially in the PROC SQL statement, and then use the RESET statement to change the same option's setting without ending the current PROC SQL step.

Restricting Row Processing with the INOBS= and OUTOBS= Options

When you are developing queries against large tables, you can reduce the time that it takes for the queries to run by reducing the number of rows that PROC SQL processes. Subsetting the tables with WHERE statements is one way to do this. Using the INOBS= and the OUTOBS= options are other ways.

The INOBS= option restricts the number of rows that PROC SQL takes as input from any single source. For example, if you specify INOBS=10, then PROC SQL uses only 10 rows from any table or view that is specified in a FROM clause. If you specify INOBS=10 and join two tables without using a WHERE clause, then the resulting table (Cartesian product) contains a maximum of 100 rows. The INOBS= option is similar to the SAS system option OBS=.

The OUTOBS= option restricts the number of rows that PROC SQL displays or writes to a table. For example, if you specify OUTOBS=10 and insert values into a table by using a query, then PROC SQL inserts a maximum of 10 rows into the resulting table. OUTOBS= is similar to the SAS data set option OBS=.

In a simple query, there might be no apparent difference between using INOBS or OUTOBS. However, at other times it is important to choose the correct option. For example, taking the average of a column with INOBS=10 returns an average of only 10 values from that column.

Limiting Iterations with the LOOPS= Option

The LOOPS= option restricts PROC SQL to the number of iterations that are specified in this option through its inner loop. By setting a limit, you can prevent queries from consuming excessive computer resources. For example, joining three large tables without meeting the join-matching conditions could create a huge internal table that would be inefficient to process. Use the LOOPS= option to prevent this from happening.

You can use the number of iterations that are reported in the SQLOOPS macro variable (after each PROC SQL statement is executed) to gauge an appropriate value for the LOOPS= option. For more information, see "Using the PROC SQL Automatic Macro Variables" on page 133.

If you use the PROMPT option with the INOBS=, OUTOBS=, or LOOPS= options, you are prompted to stop or continue processing when the limits set by these options are reached.

Checking Syntax with the NOEXEC Option and the VALIDATE Statement

To check the syntax of a PROC SQL step without actually executing it, use the NOEXEC option or the VALIDATE statement. The NOEXEC option can be used once in the PROC SQL statement, and the syntax of all queries in that PROC SQL step will be checked for accuracy without executing them. The VALIDATE statement must be specified before each SELECT statement in order for that statement to be checked for accuracy without executing. If the syntax is valid, then a message is written to the SAS log to that effect; if the syntax is invalid, then an error message is displayed. The automatic macro variable SQLRC contains an error code that indicates the validity of the syntax. For an example of the VALIDATE statement used in PROC SQL, see "Validating a Query" on page 53. For an example of using the VALIDATE statement in a SAS/AF application, see "Using the PROC SQL Automatic Macro Variables" on page 133.

Note: There is an interaction between the PROC SQL EXEC and ERRORSTOP options when SAS is running in a batch or noninteractive session. For more information, see the section about PROC SQL in the *Base SAS Procedures Guide.* △

Expanding SELECT * with the FEEDBACK Option

The FEEDBACK option expands a SELECT * (ALL) statement into the list of columns that the statement represents. Any PROC SQL view is expanded into the underlying query, and all expressions are enclosed in parentheses to indicate their order of evaluation. The FEEDBACK option also displays the resolved values of macros and macro variables.

For example, the following query is expanded in the SAS log:

```
proc sql feedback;
    select * from sql.countries;
```

Output 5.1   Expanded SELECT * Statement

```
NOTE: Statement transforms to:

      select COUNTRIES.Name, COUNTRIES.Capital, COUNTRIES.Population,
COUNTRIES.Area, COUNTRIES.Continent, COUNTRIES.UNDate
         from SQL.COUNTRIES;
```

Timing PROC SQL with the STIMER Option

Certain operations can be accomplished in more than one way. For example, there is often a join equivalent to a subquery. Consider factors such as readability and maintenance, but generally you will choose the query that runs fastest. The SAS system option STIMER shows you the cumulative time for an entire procedure. The PROC SQL STIMER option shows you how fast the individual statements in a PROC SQL step are running. This enables you to optimize your query.

Note: For the PROC SQL STIMER option to work, the SAS system option STIMER must also be specified. △

This example compares the execution times of two queries. Both queries list the names and populations of states in the UNITEDSTATES table that have a larger population than Belgium. The first query does this with a join; the second with a subquery. Output 5.2 shows the STIMER results from the SAS log.

```
proc sql stimer ;
   select us.name, us.population
      from sql.unitedstates as us, sql.countries as w
      where us.population gt w.population and
            w.name = 'Belgium';

   select Name, population
      from sql.unitedstates
      where population gt
                  (select population from sql.countries
                      where name = 'Belgium');
```

Output 5.2 Comparing Run Times of Two Queries

```
4   proc sql stimer ;
NOTE: SQL Statement used:
      real time            0.00 seconds
      cpu time             0.01 seconds

5       select us.name, us.population
6          from sql.unitedstates as us, sql.countries as w
7          where us.population gt w.population and
8                 w.name = 'Belgium';
NOTE: The execution of this query involves performing one or more Cartesian
      product joins that can not be optimized.
NOTE: SQL Statement used:
      real time            0.10 seconds
      cpu time             0.05 seconds

9
10      select Name, population
11         from sql.unitedstates
12         where population gt
13                 (select population from sql.countries
14                     where name = 'Belgium');
NOTE: SQL Statement used:
      real time            0.09 seconds
      cpu time             0.09 seconds
```

Compare the CPU time of the first query (that uses a join), 0.05 seconds, with 0.09 seconds for the second query (that uses a subquery). Although there are many factors that influence the run times of queries, generally a join runs faster than an equivalent subquery.

Resetting PROC SQL Options with the RESET Statement

Use the RESET statement to add, drop, or change the options in the PROC SQL statement. You can list the options in any order in the PROC SQL and RESET statements. Options stay in effect until they are reset.

This example first uses the NOPRINT option to prevent the SELECT statement from displaying its result table in SAS output. The RESET statement then changes the NOPRINT option to PRINT (the default) and adds the NUMBER option, which displays the row number in the result table.

```
proc sql noprint;
   title 'Countries with Population Under 20,000';
   select Name, Population from sql.countries;
reset print number;
   select Name, Population from sql.countries
      where population lt 20000;
```

Output 5.3   Resetting PROC SQL Options with the RESET Statement

```
                     Countries with Population Under 20,000

           Row  Name                              Population
           ------------------------------------------------------
             1  Leeward Islands                       12119
             2  Nauru                                 10099
             3  Turks and Caicos Islands              12119
             4  Tuvalu                                10099
             5  Vatican City                           1010
```

Improving Query Performance

There are several ways to improve query performance, including the following:

□ using indexes and composite indexes

□ using the keyword ALL in set operations when you know that there are no duplicate rows, or when it does not matter if you have duplicate rows in the result table

□ omitting the ORDER BY clause when you create tables and views

□ using in-line views instead of temporary tables (or vice versa)

□ using joins instead of subqueries

□ using WHERE expressions to limit the size of result tables that are created with joins

□ using either PROC SQL options, SAS system options, or both to replace a PUT function in a query with a logically equivalent expression

□ replacing references to the DATE, TIME, DATETIME, and TODAY functions in a query with their equivalent constant values before the query executes

□ disabling the remerging of data when summary functions are used in a query

Using Indexes to Improve Performance

Indexes are created with the CREATE INDEX statement in PROC SQL or with the MODIFY and INDEX CREATE statements in the DATASETS procedure. Indexes are stored in specialized members of a SAS library and have a SAS member type of INDEX. The values that are stored in an index are automatically updated if you make a change to the underlying data.

Indexes can improve the performance of certain classes of retrievals. For example, if an indexed column is compared to a constant value in a WHERE expression, then the index will likely improve the query's performance. Indexing the column that is specified in a correlated reference to an outer table also improves a subquery's (and hence, query's) performance. Composite indexes can improve the performance of queries that compare the columns that are named in the composite index with constant values that are linked using the AND operator. For example, if you have a compound index in the columns CITY and STATE, and the WHERE expression is specified as WHERE CITY='xxx' AND STATE='yy', then the index can be used to select that subset of rows more efficiently. Indexes can also benefit queries that have a WHERE clause in this form:

```
... where var1 in (select item1 from table1) ...
```

The values of VAR1 from the outer query are found in the inner query by using the index. An index can improve the processing of a table join, if the columns that participate in the join are indexed in one of the tables. This optimization can be done for equijoin queries only—that is, when the WHERE expression specifies that table1.X=table2.Y.

Using the Keyword ALL in Set Operations

Set operators such as UNION, OUTER UNION, EXCEPT, and INTERSECT can be used to combine queries. Specifying the optional ALL keyword prevents the final process that eliminates duplicate rows from the result table. You should use the ALL form when you know that there are no duplicate rows or when it does not matter whether the duplicate rows remain in the result table.

Omitting the ORDER BY Clause When Creating Tables and Views

If you specify the ORDER BY clause when a table or view is created, then the data is always displayed in that order unless you specify another ORDER BY clause in a query that references that table or view. As with any sorting procedure, using ORDER BY when retrieving data has certain performance costs, especially on large tables. If the order of your output is not important for your results, then your queries will typically run faster without an ORDER BY clause.

Using In-Line Views versus Temporary Tables

It is often helpful when you are exploring a problem to break a query down into several steps and create temporary tables to hold the intermediate results. After you have worked through the problem, combining the queries into one query by using in-line views can be more efficient. However, under certain circumstances it is more efficient to use temporary tables. You should try both methods to determine which is more efficient for your case.

Comparing Subqueries with Joins

Many subqueries can also be expressed as joins. Generally, a join is processed at least as efficiently as the subquery. PROC SQL stores the result values for each unique set of correlation columns temporarily, thereby eliminating the need to calculate the subquery more than once.

Using WHERE Expressions with Joins

When joining tables, you should specify a WHERE expression. Joins without WHERE expressions are often time-consuming to evaluate because of the multiplier effect of the Cartesian product. For example, joining two tables of 1,000 rows each without specifying a WHERE expression or an ON clause, produces a result table with one million rows.

PROC SQL executes and obtains the correct results in unbalanced WHERE expressions (or ON join expressions) in an equijoin, as shown here, but handles them inefficiently:

```
where table1.columnA-table2.columnB=0
```

It is more efficient to rewrite this clause to balance the expression so that columns from each table are on alternate sides of the equals condition:

```
where table1.columnA=table2.columnB
```

PROC SQL sequentially processes joins that do not have an equijoin condition evaluating each row against the WHERE expression: that is, joins without an equijoin condition are not evaluated using sort-merge or index-lookup techniques. Evaluating left and right outer joins is generally comparable to, or only slightly slower than, a standard inner join. A full outer join usually requires two passes over both tables in the join, although PROC SQL tries to store as much data as possible in buffers. Thus for small tables, an outer join might be processed with only one physical read of the data.

Optimizing the PUT Function

Reducing the PUT Function

There are several ways you can improve the performance of queries for formatted data by optimizing the PUT functions. If you reference tables in a database, eliminating references to PUT functions can enable more of the query to be passed down to the database. It can also simplify WHERE clause evaluation for the default Base SAS engine.

□ By using either the PROC SQL REDUCEPUT= option or the SQLREDUCEPUT= system option, you can specify that SAS reduces the PUT function as much as possible before the query is processed. If the query also contains a WHERE clause, the evaluation of the WHERE clause is simplified.

The following SELECT statements are examples of queries that would be reduced if you specify that optimization should occur.

```
select x, y from &lib..b where (PUT(x, abc.) in ('yes', 'no'));
select x from &lib..a where (PUT(x, udfmt.) -- trim(left('small')));
```

□ For databases that allow implicit pass-through when the row count for a table is not known, PROC SQL allows the optimization in order for the query to be executed by the database. When the PROC SQL REDUCEPUT= option or the SQLREDUCEPUT= system option is set to NONE, PROC SQL considers the value of the PROC SQL REDUCEPUTOBS= option or the SQLREDUCEPUTOBS= system option and determines whether to optimize the PUT function. The PROC SQL REDUCEPUTOBS= option or the SQLREDUCEPUTOBS= system option specifies the minimum number of rows that must be in a table in order for PROC SQL to consider optimizing the PUT function in a query. For databases that do not allow implicit pass-through, PROC SQL does not perform the optimization, and more of the query is performed by SAS.

□ Some formats, especially user-defined formats, can contain many format values. Depending on the number of matches for a given PUT function expression, the resulting expression can list many format values. If the number of format values becomes too large, the query performance can degrade. When the PROC SQL REDUCEPUT= option or the SQLREDUCEPUT= system option is set to NONE, PROC SQL considers the value of the PROC SQL REDUCEPUTVALUES= option or the SQLREDUCEPUTVALUES= system option and determines whether to optimize the PUT function in a query. For databases that do not allow implicit pass-through, PROC SQL does not perform the optimization, and more of the query is performed by SAS.

For more information, see the REDUCEPUT=, REDUCEPUTOBS=, and REDCUEPUTVALUES= options in the *Base SAS Procedures Guide*, and the SQLREDUCEPUT=, SQLREDUCEPUTOBS=, and SQLREDUCEPUTVALUES= system options in *SAS Language Reference: Dictionary*.

Note: PROC SQL can consider both the REDUCEPUTOBS= and the REDUCEPUTVALUES= options (or SQLREDUCEPUTOBS= and SQLREDUCEPUTVALUES= system options) when trying to determine whether to optimize the PUT function. △

Deploying the PUT Function and SAS Formats inside Teradata

In SAS 9.2 Phase 2 and later, if you use SAS/ACCESS for Teradata, you can use %INDTD_PUBLISH_FORMATS macro to deploy, or *publish*, the PUT function implementation to Teradata as a function named SAS_PUT( ). As with any other programming function, the SAS_PUT( ) function can take one or more input parameters and return an output value. After the SAS_PUT( ) function is deployed in Teradata and the SQLMAPPUTTO system option is set to SAS_PUT, you can use the SAS_PUT( ) function as you would use any standard SQL function *inside the database*.

In addition, the SAS_PUT( ) function supports the use of SAS formats in SQL queries that are submitted to Teradata. You also use the %INDTD_PUBLISH_FORMATS macro to publish both the formats that are supplied by SAS and the custom formats that you create with the FORMAT procedure to Teradata.

By publishing the PUT function implementation to Teradata as the SAS_PUT( ) function to support the use of SAS formats, and by packaging both the formats that are supplied by SAS and the custom formats that are defined using the FORMAT procedure, the following advantages are realized:

- □ The entire SQL query can be processed inside the database.
- □ The SAS format processing leverages the DBMS's scalable architecture.
- □ The results are grouped by the formatted data and are extracted from the Teradata database.

Note: Using both the SQLREDUCEPUT system option (or the PROC SQL REDUCEPUT= option) and the SAS_PUT( ) function can result in a significant performance boost. △

For more information about using the %INDTD_PUBLISH_FORMATS macro and the SQLMAPPUTTO system option, see *SAS/ACCESS for Relational Databases: Reference*.

Replacing References to the DATE, TIME, DATETIME, and TODAY Functions

When the PROC SQL CONSTDATETIME option or the SQLCONSTDATETIME system option is set, PROC SQL evaluates the DATE, TIME, DATETIME, and TODAY functions in a query once, and uses those values throughout the query. Computing these values once ensures consistent results when the functions are used multiple times in a query, or when the query executes the functions close to a date or time boundary. When referencing database tables, performance is enhanced because it allows more of the query to be passed down to the database.

For more information, see the CONSTDATETIME option in the *Base SAS Procedures Guide* or the SQLCONSTDATETIME system option in *SAS Language Reference: Dictionary*.

Note: If you specify both the PROC SQL REDUCEPUT option or the SQLREDUCEPUT system option and the PROC SQL CONSTDATETIME option or the

SQLCONSTDATETIME system option, PROC SQL replaces the DATE, TIME, DATETIME, and TODAY functions with their respective values in order to determine the PUT function value before the query executes. △

Disabling the Remerging of Data When Using Summary Functions

When you use a summary function in a SELECT clause or a HAVING clause, PROC SQL might remerge the data. Remerging the data involves two passes through the data. If you set the PROC SQL NOREMERGE option or the NOSQLREMERGE system option, PROC SQL will not process the remerging of data. When referencing database tables, performance is enhanced because it enables more of the query to be passed down to the database.

For more information, see the PROC SQL statement REMERGE option in the *Base SAS Procedures Guide* and the SQLREMERGE system option in *SAS Language Reference: Dictionary*.

Accessing SAS System Information by Using DICTIONARY Tables

What Are Dictionary Tables?

DICTIONARY tables are special read-only PROC SQL tables or views. They retrieve information about all the SAS libraries, SAS data sets, SAS system options, and external files that are associated with the current SAS session. For example, the DICTIONARY.COLUMNS table contains information such as name, type, length, and format, about all columns in all tables that are known to the current SAS session.

PROC SQL automatically assigns the DICTIONARY libref. To get information from DICTIONARY tables, specify DICTIONARY.*table-name* in the FROM clause in a SELECT statement in PROC SQL.

DICTIONARY.*table-name* is valid in PROC SQL only. However, SAS provides PROC SQL views, based on the DICTIONARY tables, that can be used in other SAS procedures and in the DATA step. These views are stored in the SASHELP library and are commonly called "SASHELP views."

For an example of a DICTIONARY table, see "Reporting from DICTIONARY Tables" in the *Base SAS Procedures Guide*.

The following table describes the DICTIONARY tables that are available and shows the associated SASHELP views for each table.

Table 5.1   DICTIONARY Tables and Associated SASHELP Views

DICTIONARY Table	SASHELP View	Description
CATALOGS	VCATALG	Contains information about known SAS catalogs.
CHECK_CONSTRAINTS	VCHKCON	Contains information about known check constraints.
COLUMNS	VCOLUMN	Contains information about columns in all known tables.

DICTIONARY Table	SASHELP View	Description
CONSTRAINT_COLUMN_USAGE	VCNCOLU	Contains information about columns that are referred to by integrity constraints.
CONSTRAINT_TABLE_USAGE	VCNTABU	Contains information about tables that have integrity constraints defined on them.
DATAITEMS	VDATAIT	Contains information about known information map data items.
DESTINATIONS	VDEST	Contains information about known ODS destinations.
DICTIONARIES	VDCTNRY	Contains information about all DICTIONARY tables.
ENGINES	VENGINE	Contains information about SAS engines.
EXTFILES	VEXTFL	Contains information about known external files.
FILTERS	VFILTER	Contains information about known information map filters.
FORMATS	VFORMAT VCFORMAT	Contains information about currently accessible formats and informats.
FUNCTIONS	VFUNC	Contains information about currently accessible functions.
GOPTIONS	VGOPT VALLOPT	Contains information about currently defined graphics options (SAS/GRAPH software). SASHELP.VALLOPT includes SAS system options as well as graphics options.
INDEXES	VINDEX	Contains information about known indexes.
INFOMAPS	VINFOMP	Contains information about known information maps.
LIBNAMES	VLIBNAM	Contains information about currently defined SAS libraries.
MACROS	VMACRO	Contains information about currently defined macro variables.
MEMBERS	VMEMBER VSACCES VSCATLG VSLIB VSTABLE VSTABVW VSVIEW	Contains information about all objects that are in currently defined SAS libraries. SASHELP.VMEMBER contains information for all member types; the other SASHELP views are specific to particular member types (such as tables or views).
OPTIONS	VOPTION VALLOPT	Contains information about SAS system options. SASHELP.VALLOPT includes graphics options as well as SAS system options.

DICTIONARY Table	SASHELP View	Description
REFERENTIAL_CONSTRAINTS	VREFCON	Contains information about referential constraints.
REMEMBER	VREMEMB	Contains information about known remembers.
STYLES	VSTYLE	Contains information about known ODS styles.
TABLE_CONSTRAINTS	VTABCON	Contains information about integrity constraints in all known tables.
TABLES	VTABLE	Contains information about known tables.
TITLES	VTITLE	Contains information about currently defined titles and footnotes.
VIEWS	VVIEW	Contains information about known data views.

Retrieving Information about DICTIONARY Tables and SASHELP Views

To see how each DICTIONARY table is defined, submit a DESCRIBE TABLE statement. This example shows the definition of DICTIONARY.TABLES:

```
proc sql;
   describe table dictionary.tables;
```

The results are written to the SAS log.

Output 5.4 Definition of DICTIONARY.TABLES

```
NOTE: SQL table DICTIONARY.TABLES was created like:

create table DICTIONARY.TABLES
  (
   libname char(8) label='Library Name',
   memname char(32) label='Member Name',
   memtype char(8) label='Member Type',
   dbms_memtype char(32) label='DBMS Member Type',
   memlabel char(256) label='Data Set Label',
   typemem char(8) label='Data Set Type',
   crdate num format=DATETIME informat=DATETIME label='Date Created',
   modate num format=DATETIME informat=DATETIME label='Date Modified',
   nobs num label='Number of Physical Observations',
   obslen num label='Observation Length',
   nvar num label='Number of Variables',
   protect char(3) label='Type of Password Protection',
   compress char(8) label='Compression Routine',
   encrypt char(8) label='Encryption',
   npage num label='Number of Pages',
   filesize num label='Size of File',
   pcompress num label='Percent Compression',
   reuse char(3) label='Reuse Space',
   bufsize num label='Bufsize',
   delobs num label='Number of Deleted Observations',
   nlobs num label='Number of Logical Observations',
   maxvar num label='Longest variable name',
   maxlabel num label='Longest label',
   maxgen num label='Maximum number of generations',
   gen num label='Generation number',
   attr char(3) label='Data Set Attributes',
   indxtype char(9) label='Type of Indexes',
   datarep char(32) label='Data Representation',
   sortname char(8) label='Name of Collating Sequence',
   sorttype char(4) label='Sorting Type',
   sortchar char(8) label='Charset Sorted By',
   reqvector char(24) format=$HEX48 informat=$HEX48 label='Requirements Vector',
   datarepname char(170) label='Data Representation Name',
   encoding char(256) label='Data Encoding',
   audit char(8) label='Audit Trail Active?',
   audit_before char(8) label='Audit Before Image?',
   audit_admin char(8) label='Audit Admin Image?',
   audit_error char(8) label='Audit Error Image?',
   audit_data char(8) label='Audit Data Image?',
   num_character num label='Number of Character Variables',
   num_numeric num label='Number of Numeric Variables'
  );
```

Similarly, you can use the DESCRIBE VIEW statement in PROC SQL to determine how a SASHELP view is defined. Here is an example:

```
proc sql;
   describe view sashelp.vtable;
```

Output 5.5 Description of SASHELP.VTABLE

```
NOTE: SQL view SASHELP.VSTABVW is defined as:

      select libname, memname, memtype
        from DICTIONARY.MEMBERS
       where (memtype='VIEW') or (memtype='DATA')
    order by libname asc, memname asc;
```

Using DICTIONARY.TABLES

DICTIONARY tables are commonly used to monitor and manage SAS sessions because the data is more easily manipulated than the output from other sources such as PROC DATASETS. You can query DICTIONARY tables the same way that you query any other table, including subsetting with a WHERE clause, ordering the results, and creating PROC SQL views.

Note that many character values in the DICTIONARY tables are stored as all-uppercase characters; you should design your queries accordingly.

Because DICTIONARY tables are read-only objects, you cannot insert rows or columns, alter column attributes, or add integrity constraints to them.

Note: For DICTIONARY.TABLES and SASHELP.VTABLE, if a table is read-protected with a password, then the only information that is listed for that table is the library name, member name, member type, and type of password protection. All other information is set to missing. △

Note: An error occurs if DICTIONARY.TABLES is used to retrieve information about an SQL view that exists in one library but has an input table from a second library that has not been assigned. △

The following query uses a SELECT and subsetting WHERE clause to retrieve information about permanent tables and views that appear in the SQL library:

```
proc sql;
   title 'All Tables and Views in the SQL Library';
   select libname, memname, memtype, nobs
      from dictionary.tables
      where libname='SQL';
```

Output 5.6   Tables and Views Used in This Document

```
              All Tables and Views in the SQL Library

                                              Number of
      Library                       Member    Physical
      Name      Member Name         Type      Observations
      --------------------------------------------------------------
      SQL       A                   DATA            4
      SQL       B                   DATA            3
      SQL       CITYREPORT          DATA          132
      SQL       CONTINENTS          DATA            9
      SQL       COUNTRIES           DATA          209
      SQL       DENSITIES           DATA           10
      SQL       EXTREMETEMPS        DATA           20
      SQL       FEATURES            DATA           76
      SQL       MYSTATES            DATA            0
      SQL       NEWCONTINENTS       VIEW            .
      SQL       NEWCOUNTRIES        DATA            6
      SQL       NEWPOP              DATA           14
      SQL       NEWSTATES           DATA            0
      SQL       OILPROD             DATA           31
      SQL       OILRSRVS            DATA           26
      SQL       POSTALCODES         DATA           59
      SQL       REFEREE             DATA            4
      SQL       STATECODES          DATA           51
      SQL       UNITEDSTATES        DATA           57
      SQL       USCITYCOORDS        DATA          132
      SQL       USPOSTAL            DATA            0
      SQL       WORLDCITYCOORDS     DATA          222
      SQL       WORLDCOUNTRIES      DATA          208
      SQL       WORLDTEMPS          DATA           59
```

Using DICTIONARY.COLUMNS

DICTIONARY tables are useful when you want to find specific columns to include in reports. The following query shows which of the tables that are used in this document contain the Country column:

```
proc sql;
   title 'All Tables That Contain the Country Column';
   select libname, memname, name
      from dictionary.columns
      where name='Country' and
            libname='SQL';
```

Output 5.7   Using DICTONARY.COLUMNS to Locate Specific Columns

```
              All Tables That Contain the Country Column

      Library
      Name      Member Name           Column Name
      ------------------------------------------------------------------
      SQL       OILPROD               Country
      SQL       OILRSRVS              Country
      SQL       WORLDCITYCOORDS       Country
      SQL       WORLDTEMPS            Country
```

DICTIONARY Tables and Performance

When querying a DICTIONARY table, SAS launches a discovery process that gathers information that is pertinent to that table. Depending on the DICTIONARY table that is being queried, this discovery process can search libraries, open tables, and execute views. Unlike other SAS procedures and the DATA step, PROC SQL can mitigate this process by optimizing the query before the discovery process is launched. Therefore, although it is possible to access DICTIONARY table information with SAS procedures or the DATA step by using the SASHELP views, it is often more efficient to use PROC SQL instead.

Note: You cannot use data set options with DICTIONARY tables. △

For example, the following programs produce the same result, but the PROC SQL step runs much faster because the WHERE clause is processed before the tables that are referenced by the SASHELP.VCOLUMN view are opened:

```
data mytable;
   set sashelp.vcolumn;
   where libname='WORK' and memname='SALES';
run;
```

```
proc sql;
   create table mytable as
      select * from sashelp.vcolumn
      where libname='WORK' and memname='SALES';
quit;
```

Note: SAS does not maintain DICTIONARY table information between queries. Each query of a DICTIONARY table launches a new discovery process. △

If you are querying the same DICTIONARY table several times in a row, then you can get even faster performance by creating a temporary SAS data set (with the DATA step SET statement or the PROC SQL CREATE TABLE AS statement) with the information that you want and running your query against that data set.

When you query DICTIONARY.TABLES or SASHELP.VTABLE, all the tables and views in all the libraries that are assigned to the SAS session are opened to retrieve the requested information.

You can use a WHERE clause to help restrict which libraries are searched. However, the WHERE clause will not process most function calls such as UPCASE.

For example, if **where UPCASE (libname) ='WORK'** is used, the UPCASE function prevents the WHERE clause from optimizing this condition. All libraries that are assigned to the SAS session are searched. Searching all the libraries could cause an unexpected increase in search time, depending on the number of libraries that are assigned to the SAS session.

The DICTIONARY information for LIBNAME and MEMNAME values is stored in uppercase. If you supply values for LIBNAME and MEMNAME values in uppercase; that is, if you remove the UPCASE function, the WHERE clause will be optimized and performance will be improved. In the previous example, the code would be changed to **where libname='WORK'**.

Note: If you query table information from a library that is assigned to an external database and you use the LIBNAME statement PRESERVE_TAB_NAMES=YES option, you should supply the LIBNAME and MEMNAME values in uppercase and place the MEMNAME keyword in the UPCASE function.

If you query column information from a library that is assigned to an external database and you use the LIBNAME statement PRESERVE_COL_NAMES=YES option, you should supply the NAME value in uppercase and place the NAME keyword in the UPCASE function. △

Using SAS Data Set Options with PROC SQL

In PROC SQL, you can apply most of the SAS data set options, such as KEEP= and DROP=, to tables or SAS/ACCESS views any time that you specify a table or SAS/ACCESS view. In the SQL procedure, SAS data set options that are separated by spaces are enclosed in parentheses. The data set options immediately follow the table or SAS/ACCESS view name. In the following PROC SQL step, the RENAME= data set option renames LNAME to LASTNAME for the STAFF1 table. The OBS= data set option restricts the number of rows that are read from STAFF1 to 15:

```
proc sql;
   create table
         staff1(rename=(lname=lastname)) as
      select *
         from staff(obs=15);
```

SAS data set options can be combined with SQL statement arguments. In the following PROC SQL step, the PW= data set option assigns a password to the TEST table, and the ALTER= data set option assigns an alter password to the STAFF1 table:

```
proc sql;
   create table test
      (a character, b numeric, pw=cat);
   create index staffidx on
      staff1 (lastname, alter=dog);
```

In this PROC SQL step, the PW= data set option assigns a password to the ONE table. The password is used when inserting a row and updating the table.

```
proc sql;
    create table one(pw=red, col1 num, col2 num, col3 num);
   quit;

proc sql;
   insert into one(pw=red, col1, col3)
   values(1, 3);
quit;
proc sql;
   update one(pw=red)
      set col2 = 22
         where col2 = . ;
quit;
```

You cannot use SAS data set options with DICTIONARY tables because DICTIONARY tables are read-only objects.

The only SAS data set options that you can use with PROC SQL views are data set options that assign and provide SAS passwords: READ=, WRITE=, ALTER=, and PW=.

For more information about SAS data set options, see *SAS Language Reference: Dictionary*.

Using PROC SQL with the SAS Macro Facility

The macro facility is a programming tool that you can use to extend and customize SAS software. The macro facility reduces the amount of text that you must enter to perform common or repeated tasks and improves the efficiency and usefulness of your SQL programs.

The macro facility enables you to assign a name to character strings or groups of SAS programming statements. Thereafter, you can work with the names rather than with the text itself. For more information about the SAS macro facility, see *SAS Macro Language: Reference*.

Macro variables provide an efficient way to replace text strings in SAS code. The macro variables that you create and name are called *user-defined macro variables*. The macros variables that are defined by SAS are called *automatic macro variables*. PROC SQL produces six automatic macro variables (SQLOBS, SQLRC, SQLOOPS, SQLEXITCODE, SQLXRC, and SQLXMSG) to help you troubleshoot your programs. For more information, see "Using the PROC SQL Automatic Macro Variables" on page 133.

Creating Macro Variables in PROC SQL

Other software vendors' SQL products allow the embedding of SQL into another language. References to variables (columns) of that language are termed *host-variable references*. They are differentiated from references to columns in tables by names that are prefixed with a colon. The host-variable stores the values of the object-items that are listed in the SELECT clause.

The only host language that is currently available in SAS is the macro language, which is part of Base SAS software. When a calculation is performed on a column's value, its result can be stored, using *:macro-variable*, in the macro facility. The result can then be referenced by that name in another PROC SQL query or SAS procedure. Host-variable can be used only in the outer query of a SELECT statement, not in a subquery. Host-variable cannot be used in a CREATE statement.

If the query produces more than one row of output, then the macro variable will contain only the value from the first row. If the query has no rows in its output, then the macro variable is not modified. If the macro variable does not exist yet, it will not be created. The PROC SQL macro variable SQLOBS contains the number of rows that are produced by the query.

Note: The SQLOBS automatic macro variable is assigned a value *after* the SQL SELECT statement executes. △

Creating Macro Variables from the First Row of a Query Result

If you specify a single macro variable in the INTO clause, then PROC SQL assigns the variable the value from the first row only of the appropriate column in the SELECT list. In this example, &country1 is assigned the value from the first row of the Country column, and &barrels1 is assigned the value from the first row of the Barrels column. The NOPRINT option prevents PROC SQL from displaying the results of the query. The %PUT statement writes the contents of the macro variables to the SAS log.

```
proc sql noprint;
    select country, barrels
        into :country1, :barrels1
        from sql.oilrsrvs;
```

```
%put &country1 &barrels1;
```

Output 5.8 Creating Macro Variables from the First Row of a Query Result

```
4   proc sql noprint;
5      select country, barrels
6         into :country1, :barrels1
7         from sql.oilrsrvs;
8
9   %put &country1 &barrels1;
Algeria                          9,200,000,000
NOTE: PROCEDURE SQL used:
      real time           0.12 seconds
```

Creating a Macro Variable from the Result of an Aggregate Function

A useful feature of macro variables is that they enable you to display data values in SAS titles. The following example prints a subset of the WORLDTEMPS table and lists the highest temperature in Canada in the title:

```
proc sql outobs=12;
   reset noprint;
   select max(AvgHigh)
      into :maxtemp
      from sql.worldtemps
      where country = 'Canada';
reset print;
   title "The Highest Temperature in Canada: &maxtemp";
   select city, AvgHigh format 4.1
      from sql.worldtemps
      where country = 'Canada';
```

Note: You must use double quotation marks in the TITLE statement to resolve the reference to the macro variable. △

Output 5.9 Including a Macro Variable Reference in the Title

```
            The Highest Temperature in Canada:      80

                                       Avg
                        City          High
                        -----------------------
                        Montreal       77.0
                        Quebec         76.0
                        Toronto        80.0
```

Creating Multiple Macro Variables

You can create one new macro variable per row from the result of a SELECT statement. Use the keywords THROUGH, THRU, or a hyphen (-) in an INTO clause to create a range of macro variables.

Note: When you specify a range of macro variables, the SAS macro facility creates only the number of macro variables that are needed. For example, if you specify

:var1-:var9999 and only 55 variables are needed, only **:var1-:var55** is created. The SQLOBS automatic variable is useful if a subsequent part of your program needs to know how many variables were actually created. In this example, SQLOBS would have a value of 55. △

This example assigns values to macro variables from the first four rows of the Name column and the first three rows of the Population column. The %PUT statements write the results to the SAS log.

```
proc sql noprint;
    select name, Population
        into :country1 - :country4, :pop1 - :pop3
            from sql.countries;

%put &country1 &pop1;
%put &country2 &pop2;
%put &country3 &pop3;
%put &country4;
```

Output 5.10   Creating Multiple Macro Variables

```
4  proc sql noprint;
5     select name, Population
6         into :country1 - :country4, :pop1 - :pop3
7         from sql.countries;
8
9  %put &country1 &pop1;
Afghanistan 17070323
10  %put &country2 &pop2;
Albania 3407400
11  %put &country3 &pop3;
Algeria 28171132
12  %put &country4;
Andorra
```

Concatenating Values in Macro Variables

You can concatenate the values of one column into one macro variable. This form is useful for building a list of variables or constants. Use the SEPARATED BY keywords to specify a character to delimit the values in the macro variable.

This example assigns the first five values from the Name column of the COUNTRIES table to the &countries macro variable. The INOBS option limits PROC SQL to using the first five rows of the COUNTRIES table. A comma and a space are used to delimit the values in the macro variable.

```
proc sql noprint inobs=5;
    select Name
        into :countries separated by ', '
        from sql.countries;

%put &countries;
```

Output 5.11   Concatenating Values in Macro Variables

```
4  proc sql noprint inobs=5;
5     select Name
6        into :countries separated by ', '
7           from sql.countries;
WARNING: Only 5 records were read from SQL.COUNTRIES due to INOBS= option.
8
9  %put &countries;
Afghanistan, Albania, Algeria, Andorra, Angola
```

The leading and trailing blanks are trimmed from the values before the macro
variables are created. If you do not want the blanks to be trimmed, then add NOTRIM
to the INTO clause. Here is the previous example with NOTRIM added:

```
proc sql noprint inobs=5;
   select Name
      into :countries separated by ',' NOTRIM
      from sql.countries;


%put &countries;
```

Output 5.12   Concatenating Values in Macro Variables—Blanks Not Removed

```
1     proc sql noprint inobs=5;
2        select Name
3           into :countries separated by ',' NOTRIM
4           from sql.countries;
WARNING: Only 5 records were read from SQL.COUNTRIES due to INOBS= option.
5
6     %put &countries;
Afghanistan                           ,Albania                           ,Algeria
                         ,Andorra                           ,Angola
```

Defining Macros to Create Tables

Macros are useful as interfaces for table creation. You can use the SAS macro facility
to help you create new tables and add rows to existing tables.

The following example creates a table that lists people to serve as referees for
reviews of academic papers. No more than three people per subject are allowed in a
table. The macro that is defined in this example checks the number of referees before it
inserts a new referee's name into the table. The macro has two parameters: the
referee's name and the subject matter of the academic paper.

```
proc sql;
create table sql.referee
   (Name      char(15),
    Subject   char(15));

   /* define the macro */
%macro addref(name,subject);
%local count;

   /* are there three referees in the table? */
```

```
   reset noprint;
      select count(*)
         into :count
         from sql.referee
         where subject="&subject";

%if &count ge 3 %then %do;
   reset print;
   title "ERROR: &name not inserted for subject -- &subject..";
   title2 "          There are 3 referees already.";
   select * from sql.referee where subject="&subject";
   reset noprint;
   %end;

%else %do;
   insert into sql.referee(name,subject) values("&name","&subject");
   %put NOTE: &name has been added for subject -- &subject..;
   %end;

%mend;
```

Submit the %ADDREF() macro with its two parameters to add referee names to the table. Each time you submit the macro, a message is written to the SAS log.

```
%addref(Conner,sailing);
%addref(Fay,sailing);
%addref(Einstein,relativity);
%addref(Smythe,sailing);
%addref(Naish,sailing);
```

Output 5.13 Defining Macros to Create Tables

```
34  %addref(Conner,sailing);
NOTE: 1 row was inserted into SQL.REFEREE.

NOTE: Conner has been added for subject - sailing.
35  %addref(Fay,sailing);
NOTE: 1 row was inserted into SQL.REFEREE.

NOTE: Fay has been added for subject - sailing.
36  %addref(Einstein,relativity);
NOTE: 1 row was inserted into SQL.REFEREE.

NOTE: Einstein has been added for subject - relativity.
37  %addref(Smythe,sailing);
NOTE: 1 row was inserted into SQL.REFEREE.

NOTE: Smythe has been added for subject - sailing.
38  %addref(Naish,sailing);
```

The output has a row added with each execution of the %ADDREF() macro. When the table contains three referee names, it is displayed in SAS output with the message that it can accept no more referees.

Output 5.14 Result Table and Message Created with SAS Macro Language Interface

```
           ERROR: Naish not inserted for subject - sailing.
                  There are 3 referees already.

           Name           Subject
           ------------------------------
           Conner         sailing
           Fay            sailing
           Smythe         sailing
```

Using the PROC SQL Automatic Macro Variables

PROC SQL sets up macro variables with certain values after it executes each statement. These macro variables can be tested inside a macro to determine whether to continue executing the PROC SQL step.

After each PROC SQL statement has executed, the following macro variables are updated with these values:

SQLEXITCODE
: contains the highest return code that occurred from some types of SQL insert failures. This return code is written to the SYSERR macro variable when PROC SQL terminates.

SQLOBS
: contains the number of rows that were processed by an SQL procedure statement. For example, the SQLOBS macro variable contains the number of rows that were formatted and displayed in SAS output by a SELECT statement or the number of rows that were deleted by a DELETE statement.

: When the NOPRINT option is specified, the value of the SQLOBS macro variable depends on whether an output table, single macro variable, macro variable list, or macro variable range is created:

  □ If no output table, macro variable list, or macro variable range is created, then SQLOBS contains the value 1.

  □ If an output table is created, then SQLOBS contains the number of rows in the output table.

  □ If a single macro variable is created, then SQLOBS contains the value 1.

  □ If a macro variable list or macro variable range is created, then SQLOBS contains the number of rows that are processed to create the macro variable list or range.

: If an SQL view is created, then SQLOBS contains the value 0.

: *Note:* The SQLOBS automatic macro variable is assigned a value *after* the SQL SELECT statement executes. △

SQLOOPS
: contains the number of iterations that the inner loop of PROC SQL processes. The number of iterations increases proportionally with the complexity of the query. For more information, see "Limiting Iterations with the LOOPS= Option" on page 113 and the LOOPS= option in the *Base SAS Procedures Guide*.

SQLRC
contains the following status values that indicate the success of the SQL procedure statement:

0

PROC SQL statement completed successfully with no errors.

4

PROC SQL statement encountered a situation for which it issued a warning. The statement continued to execute.

8

PROC SQL statement encountered an error. The statement stopped execution at this point.

12

PROC SQL statement encountered an internal error, indicating a bug in PROC SQL that should be reported to SAS Technical Support. These errors can occur only during compile time.

16

PROC SQL statement encountered a user error. For example, this error code is used, when a subquery (that can return only a single value) evaluates to more than one row. These errors can be detected only during run time.

24

PROC SQL statement encountered a system error. For example, this error is used, if the system cannot write to a PROC SQL table because the disk is full. These errors can occur only during run time.

28

PROC SQL statement encountered an internal error, indicating a bug in PROC SQL that should be reported to SAS Technical Support. These errors can occur only during run time.

The value of SQLRC can vary based on the value of the PROC SQL statement UNDO_POLICY= option or the SQLUNDOPOLICY system option.

For example, the values for the SQLRC return code differ based on the value of the UNDO_POLICY= option or the SQLUNDOPOLICY system option if you attempt to insert duplicate values into an index that is defined using the CREATE UNIQUE INDEX statement:

☐ If you set the UNDO_POLICY= option or the SQLUNDOPOLICY system option to either REQUIRED or OPTIONAL, and you attempt to insert a duplicate index value, SAS creates and tries to maintain a copy of the table before and after updates are applied. SAS detects an error condition and supplies a return code to PROC SQL, which stops execution as soon as the error condition is received. SQLRC contains the value 24.

☐ If you set the UNDO_POLICY= option or the SQLUNDOPOLICY system option to NONE and you attempt to insert a duplicate index value, SAS does not create a before-and-after copy of the table. SAS does not detect an error condition and does not supply a return code to PROC SQL, which attempts to continue to process the updates. SQLRC contains the value 8.

SQLXMSG
contains descriptive information and the DBMS-specific return code for the error that is returned by the Pass-Through Facility.

Note: Because the value of the SQLXMSG macro variable can contain special characters (such as &, %, /, *, and ;), use the %SUPERQ macro function when printing the following value:

```
%put %superq(sqlxmsg);
```

For information about the %SUPERQ function, see *SAS Macro Language: Reference.* △

SQLXRC
   contains the DBMS-specific return code that is returned by the Pass-Through Facility.

Macro variables that are generated by PROC SQL follow the scoping rules for %LET. For more information about macro variable scoping, see *SAS Macro Language: Reference.*

Users of SAS/AF software can access these automatic macro variables in SAS Component Language (SCL) programs by using the SYMGET function. The following example uses the VALIDATE statement in a SAS/AF software application to check the syntax of a block of code. Before it issues the CREATE VIEW statement, the application checks that the view is accessible.

```
submit sql immediate;
   validate &viewdef;
end submit;

if symget('SQLRC') gt 4 then
   do;
       ... the view is not valid ...
   end;
else do;
   submit sql immediate;
      create view &viewname as &viewdef;
   end submit;
end;
```

The following example retrieves the data from the COUNTRIES table, but does not display the table because the NOPRINT option is specified in the PROC SQL statement. The %PUT macro language statement displays the three automatic macro variable values in the SAS log. For more information about the %PUT statement and the SAS macro facility, see *SAS Macro Language: Reference.*

```
proc sql noprint;
   select * from sql.countries;
%put SQLOBS=*&sqlobs* SQLOOPS=*&sqloops* SQLRC=*&sqlrc*;
```

Output 5.15 Using the PROC SQL Automatic Macro Variables

```
SQLOBS=*1* SQLOOPS=*11* SQLRC=*0*
```

Notice that the value of SQLOBS is 1. When the NOPRINT option is used and no table or macro variables are created, SQLOBS returns a value of 1 because only one row is processed.

Note: You can use the _AUTOMATIC_ option in the %PUT statement to list the values of all automatic macro variables. The list depends on the SAS products that are installed at your site. △

Formatting PROC SQL Output by Using the REPORT Procedure

SQL provides limited output formatting capabilities. Some SQL vendors add output formatting statements to their products to address these limitations. SAS has reporting tools that enhance the appearance of PROC SQL output.

For example, SQL cannot display only the first occurrence of a repeating value in a column in its output. The following example lists cities in the USCITYCOORDS table. Notice the repeating values in the State column.

```
proc sql outobs=10;
    title 'US Cities';
    select State, City, latitude, Longitude
        from sql.uscitycoords
        order by state;
```

Output 5.16   USCITYCOORDS Table Showing Repeating State Values

```
                              US Cities

            State  City              Latitude  Longitude
            ------------------------------------------------
            AK     Sitka                  57       -135
            AK     Anchorage              61       -150
            AK     Nome                   64       -165
            AK     Juneau                 58       -134
            AL     Mobile                 31        -88
            AL     Montgomery             32        -86
            AL     Birmingham             33        -87
            AR     Hot Springs            34        -93
            AR     Little Rock            35        -92
            AZ     Flagstaff              35       -112
```

The following code uses PROC REPORT to format the output so that the state codes appear only once for each state group. A WHERE clause subsets the data so that the report lists the coordinates of cities in Pacific Rim states only. For more information about PROC REPORT, see the *Base SAS Procedures Guide*.

```
proc sql noprint;
    create table sql.cityreport as
    select *
        from sql.uscitycoords
        group by state;

proc report data=sql.cityreport
            headline
            headskip;
    title 'Coordinates of U.S. Cities in Pacific Rim States';
    column state city ('Coordinates' latitude longitude);
    define state / order format=$2. width=5 'State';
    define city / order format=$15. width=15 'City';
    define latitude / display format=4. width=8 'Latitude';
    define longitude / display format=4. width=9 'Longitude';
    where state='AK' or
          state='HI' or
```

```
                    state='WA' or
                    state='OR' or
                    state='CA';
         run;
```

Output 5.17   PROC REPORT Output Showing the First Occurrence Only of Each State Value

```
              Coordinates of U.S. Cities in Pacific Rim States

                                           Coordinates
                    State   City        Latitude  Longitude
                    -------------------------------------------

                    AK      Anchorage        61      -150
                            Juneau           58      -134
                            Nome             64      -165
                            Sitka            57      -135
                    CA      El Centro        32      -115
                            Fresno           37      -120
                            Long Beach       34      -118
                            Los Angeles      34      -118
                            Oakland          38      -122
                            Sacramento       38      -121
                            San Diego        33      -117
                            San Francisco    38      -122
                            San Jose         37      -122
                    HI      Honolulu         21      -158
                    OR      Baker            45      -118
                            Eugene           44      -124
                            Klamath Falls    42      -122
                            Portland         45      -123
                            Salem            45      -123
                    WA      Olympia          47      -123
                            Seattle          47      -122
                            Spokane          48      -117
```

Accessing a DBMS with SAS/ACCESS Software

SAS/ACCESS software for relational databases provides an interface between SAS software and data in other vendors' database management systems (DBMSs). SAS/ACCESS software provides dynamic access to DBMS data through the SAS/ACCESS LIBNAME statement and the PROC SQL Pass-Through Facility. The LIBNAME statement enables you to assign SAS librefs to DBMS objects such as schemas and databases. The Pass-Through Facility enables you to interact with a DBMS by using its SQL syntax without leaving your SAS session.

It is recommended that you use the SAS/ACCESS LIBNAME statement to access your DBMS data because it is usually the fastest and most direct method of accessing DBMS data. The LIBNAME statement offers the following advantages:

☐ Significantly fewer lines of SAS code are required to perform operations in your DBMS. For example, a single LIBNAME statement establishes a connection to your DBMS, enables you to specify how your data is processed, and enables you to easily browse your DBMS tables in SAS.

☐ You do not need to know your DBMS's SQL language to access and manipulate your DBMS data. You can use SAS procedures, such as PROC SQL, or DATA step programming on any libref that references DBMS data. You can read, insert, update, delete, and append data, as well as create and drop DBMS tables by using normal SAS syntax.

☐ The LIBNAME statement provides more control over DBMS operations such as locking, spooling, and data type conversion through the many LIBNAME options and data set options.

☐ The LIBNAME engine optimizes the processing of joins and WHERE clauses by passing these operations directly to the DBMS to take advantage of the indexing and other processing capabilities of your DBMS.

An exception to this recommendation occurs when you need to use SQL that does not conform to the ANSI standard. The SAS/ACCESS LIBNAME statement accepts only ANSI-standard SQL, but the PROC SQL Pass-Through Facility accepts all the extensions to SQL that are provided by your DBMS. Another advantage of this access method is that Pass-Through Facility statements enable the DBMS to optimize queries when the queries have summary functions (such as AVG and COUNT), GROUP BY clauses, or columns that were created by expressions (such as the COMPUTED function).

For more information about SAS/ACCESS software, see *SAS/ACCESS for Relational Databases: Reference*.

Connecting to a DBMS by Using the LIBNAME Statement

Use the LIBNAME statement to read from and write to a DBMS object as if it were a SAS data set. After connecting to a DBMS table or view by using the LIBNAME statement, you can use PROC SQL to interact with the DBMS data.

For many DBMSs, you can directly access DBMS data by assigning a libref to the DBMS by using the SAS/ACCESS LIBNAME statement. Once you have associated a libref with the DBMS, you can specify a DBMS table in a two-level SAS name and work with the table like any SAS data set. You can also embed the LIBNAME statement in a PROC SQL view (see the CREATE VIEW statement in the *Base SAS Procedures Guide*).

PROC SQL takes advantage of the capabilities of a DBMS by passing it certain operations whenever possible. For example, before implementing a join, PROC SQL checks to determine whether the DBMS can perform the join. If it can, then PROC SQL passes the join to the DBMS, which enhances performance by reducing data movement and translation. If the DBMS cannot perform the join, then PROC SQL processes the join. Using the SAS/ACCESS LIBNAME statement can often provide you with the performance benefits of the SQL Procedure Pass-Through Facility without writing DBMS-specific code.

Note: You can use the DBIDIRECTEXEC system option to send a PROC SQL CREATE TABLE AS SELECT statement or a DELETE statement directly to the database for execution, which could result in CPU and I/O performance improvement. For more information, see the SAS/ACCESS documentation for your DBMS. △

To use the SAS/ACCESS LIBNAME statement, you must have SAS/ACCESS software installed for your DBMS. For more information about the SAS/ACCESS LIBNAME statement, see the SAS/ACCESS documentation for your DBMS.

Querying a DBMS Table

This example uses PROC SQL to query the ORACLE table PAYROLL. The PROC SQL query retrieves all job codes and provides a total salary amount for each job code.

```
libname mydblib oracle user=user-id password=password
        path=path-name schema=schema-name;
```

```
proc sql;
   select jobcode label='Jobcode',
          sum(salary) as total
          label='Total for Group'
          format=dollar11.2
      from mydblib.payroll
      group by jobcode;
quit;
```

Output 5.18 Output from Querying a DBMS Table

```
                            Total for
           Jobcode             Group

               BCK        $232,148.00
               FA1        $253,433.00
               FA2        $447,790.00
               FA3        $230,537.00
               ME1        $228,002.00
               ME2        $498,076.00
               ME3        $296,875.00
               NA1        $210,161.00
               NA2        $157,149.00
               PT1        $543,264.00
               PT2        $879,252.00
               PT3         $21,009.00
               SCP        $128,162.00
               TA1        $249,492.00
               TA2        $671,499.00
               TA3        $476,155.00
```

Creating a PROC SQL View of a DBMS Table

PROC SQL views are stored query expressions that read data values from their underlying files, which can include SAS/ACCESS views of DBMS data. While DATA step views of DBMS data can be used only to read the data, PROC SQL views of DBMS data can be used to update the underlying data if the following conditions are met:

□ The PROC SQL view is based on only one DBMS table (or on a DBMS view that is based on only one DBMS table).

□ The PROC SQL view has no calculated fields.

The following example uses the LIBNAME statement to connect to an ORACLE database, create a temporary PROC SQL view of the ORACLE table SCHEDULE, and print the view by using the PRINT procedure. The LIBNAME engine optimizes the processing of joins and WHERE clauses by passing these operations directly to the DBMS to take advantage of DBMS indexing and processing capabilities.

```
libname mydblib oracle user=user-id password=password
proc sql;
   create view LON as
   select flight, dates, idnum
      from mydblib.schedule
      where dest='LON';
quit;
```

```
proc print data=work.LON noobs;
run;
```

Output 5.19   Output from the PRINT Procedure

```
FLIGHT              DATES      IDNUM

 219      04MAR1998:00:00:00    1739
 219      04MAR1998:00:00:00    1478
 219      04MAR1998:00:00:00    1130
 219      04MAR1998:00:00:00    1125
 219      04MAR1998:00:00:00    1983
 219      04MAR1998:00:00:00    1332
 219      05MAR1998:00:00:00    1428
 219      05MAR1998:00:00:00    1442
 219      05MAR1998:00:00:00    1422
 219      05MAR1998:00:00:00    1413
 219      05MAR1998:00:00:00    1574
 219      05MAR1998:00:00:00    1332
 219      06MAR1998:00:00:00    1106
 219      06MAR1998:00:00:00    1118
 219      06MAR1998:00:00:00    1425
 219      06MAR1998:00:00:00    1434
 219      06MAR1998:00:00:00    1555
 219      06MAR1998:00:00:00    1332
```

Connecting to a DBMS by Using the SQL Procedure Pass-Through Facility

What Is the Pass-Through Facility?

The SQL Procedure Pass-Through Facility enables you to send DBMS-specific SQL statements directly to a DBMS for execution. The Pass-Through Facility uses a SAS/ACCESS interface engine to connect to the DBMS. Therefore, you must have SAS/ACCESS software installed for your DBMS.

You submit SQL statements that are DBMS-specific. For example, you pass Transact-SQL statements to a Sybase database. The Pass-Through Facility's basic syntax is the same for all the DBMSs. Only the statements that are used to connect to the DBMS and the SQL statements are DBMS-specific.

With the Pass-Through Facility, you can perform the following tasks:

□ Establish a connection with the DBMS by using a CONNECT statement and terminate the connection with the DISCONNECT statement.

□ Send nonquery DBMS-specific SQL statements to the DBMS by using the EXECUTE statement.

□ Retrieve data from the DBMS to be used in a PROC SQL query with the CONNECTION TO component in a SELECT statement's FROM clause.

You can use the Pass-Through Facility statements in a query, or you can store them in a PROC SQL view. When a view is stored, any options that are specified in the corresponding CONNECT statement are also stored. Thus, when the PROC SQL view is used in a SAS program, SAS can automatically establish the appropriate connection to the DBMS.

For more information, see the CONNECT statement , the DISCONNECT statement, the EXECUTE statement, and the CONNECTION TO statement in the *Base SAS Procedures Guide*, and "The Pass-Through Facility for Relational Databases" in *SAS/ACCESS for Relational Databases: Reference.*

Note: SAS procedures that perform multipass processing cannot operate on PROC SQL views that store Pass-Through Facility statements, because the Pass-Through Facility does not allow reopening of a table after the first record has been retrieved. To work around this limitation, create a SAS data set from the view and use the SAS data set as the input data set. △

Return Codes

As you use PROC SQL statements that are available in the Pass-Through Facility, any errors are written to the SAS log. The return codes and messages that are generated by the Pass-Through Facility are available to you through the SQLXRC and SQLXMSG macro variables. Both macro variables are described in "Using the PROC SQL Automatic Macro Variables" on page 133.

Pass-Through Example

In this example, SAS/ACCESS connects to an ORACLE database by using the alias **ora2**, selects all rows in the STAFF table, and displays the first 15 rows of data by using PROC SQL.

```
proc sql outobs=15;
   connect to oracle as ora2 (user=user-id password=password);
   select * from connection to ora2 (select lname, fname, state from staff);
   disconnect from ora2;
quit;
```

Output 5.20 Output from the Pass-Through Facility Example

```
  LNAME             FNAME            STATE
  --------------------------------------------
  ADAMS             GERALD           CT
  ALIBRANDI         MARIA            CT
  ALHERTANI         ABDULLAH         NY
  ALVAREZ           MERCEDES         NY
  ALVAREZ           CARLOS           NJ
  BAREFOOT          JOSEPH           NJ
  BAUCOM            WALTER           NY
  BANADYGA          JUSTIN           CT
  BLALOCK           RALPH            NY
  BALLETTI          MARIE            NY
  BOWDEN            EARL             CT
  BRANCACCIO        JOSEPH           NY
  BREUHAUS          JEREMY           NY
  BRADY             CHRISTINE        CT
  BREWCZAK          JAKOB            CT
```

Updating PROC SQL and SAS/ACCESS Views

You can update PROC SQL and SAS/ACCESS views by using the INSERT, DELETE, and UPDATE statements, under the following conditions:

□ If the view accesses a DBMS table, then you must have been granted the appropriate authorization by the external database management system (for example, DB2). You must have installed the SAS/ACCESS software for your DBMS. For more information about SAS/ACCESS views, see the SAS/ACCESS interface guide for your DBMS.

□ You can update only a single table through a view. The table cannot be joined to another table or linked to another table with a set-operator. The view cannot contain a subquery.

□ You can update a column in a view by using the column's alias, but you cannot update a derived column—that is, a column that is produced by an expression. In the following example, you can update the column SS, but not WeeklySalary:

```
create view EmployeeSalaries as
    select Employee, SSNumber as SS,
           Salary/52 as WeeklySalary
           from employees;
```

□ You cannot update a view that contains an ORDER BY.

Note: Beginning with SAS 9, PROC SQL views, the Pass-Through Facility, and the SAS/ACCESS LIBNAME statement are the preferred ways to access relational DBMS data. SAS/ACCESS views are no longer recommended. You can convert existing SAS/ACCESS views to PROC SQL views by using the CV2VIEW procedure. For more information, see the CV2VIEW Procedure in *SAS/ACCESS for Relational Databases: Reference.* △

Using the Output Delivery System with PROC SQL

The Output Delivery System (ODS) enables you to produce the output from PROC SQL in a variety of different formats such as PostScript, HTML, or list output. ODS defines the structure of the raw output from SAS procedures and from the SAS DATA step. The combination of data with a definition of its output structure is called an *output object*. Output objects can be sent to any of the various ODS destinations, which include listing, HTML, output, and printer. When new destinations are added to ODS, they automatically become available to PROC SQL, to all other SAS procedures that support ODS, and to the DATA step. For more information about ODS, see the *SAS Output Delivery System: User's Guide.*

The following example opens the HTML destination and specifies ODSOUT.HTM as the file that will contain the HTML output. The output from PROC SQL is sent to ODSOUT.HTM.

Note: This example uses filenames that might not be valid in all operating environments. To run the example successfully in your operating environment, you might need to change the file specifications. △

Note: Some browsers require an extension of HTM or HTML on the filename. △

```
ods html body='odsout.htm';
    proc sql outobs=12;
```

```
       title 'Coordinates of U.S. Cities';
       select *
          from sql.uscitycoords;
ods html close;
```

Display 5.1   ODS HTML Output

Coordinates of U.S. Cities

City	State	Latitude	Longitude
Albany	NY	43	-74
Albuquerque	NM	36	-106
Amarillo	TX	35	-102
Anchorage	AK	61	-150
Annapolis	MD	39	-77
Atlanta	GA	34	-84
Augusta	ME	44	-70
Austin	TX	30	-98
Baker	OR	45	-118
Baltimore	MD	39	-76
Bangor	ME	45	-69
Baton Rouge	LA	31	-91

6

Practical Problem-Solving with PROC SQL

Overview   **146**
Computing a Weighted Average   **146**
   Problem   **146**
   Background Information   **146**
   Solution   **147**
   How It Works   **147**
Comparing Tables   **148**
   Problem   **148**
   Background Information   **148**
   Solution   **149**
   How It Works   **149**
Overlaying Missing Data Values   **150**
   Problem   **150**
   Background Information   **150**
   Solution   **150**
   How It Works   **151**
Computing Percentages within Subtotals   **152**
   Problem   **152**
   Background Information   **152**
   Solution   **152**
   How It Works   **153**
Counting Duplicate Rows in a Table   **153**
   Problem   **153**
   Background Information   **153**
   Solution   **154**
   How It Works   **154**
Expanding Hierarchical Data in a Table   **155**
   Problem   **155**
   Background Information   **155**
   Solution   **155**
   How It Works   **156**
Summarizing Data in Multiple Columns   **157**
   Problem   **157**
   Background Information   **157**
   Solution   **157**
   How It Works   **158**
Creating a Summary Report   **158**
   Problem   **158**
   Background Information   **158**
   Solution   **159**
   How It Works   **160**

Creating a Customized Sort Order **161**
    Problem **161**
    Background Information **161**
    Solution **161**
    How It Works **162**
Conditionally Updating a Table **163**
    Problem **163**
    Background Information **163**
    Solution **163**
    How It Works **164**
Updating a Table with Values from Another Table **165**
    Problem **165**
    Background Information **165**
    Solution **166**
    How It Works **167**
Creating and Using Macro Variables **167**
    Problem **167**
    Background Information **167**
    Solution **167**
    How It Works **170**
Using PROC SQL Tables in Other SAS Procedures **170**
    Problem **170**
    Background Information **170**
    Solution **171**
    How It Works **173**

Overview

This section shows you examples of solutions that PROC SQL can provide. Each example includes a statement of the problem to solve, background information that you must know to solve the problem, the PROC SQL solution code, and an explanation of how the solution works.

Computing a Weighted Average

Problem

You want to compute a weighted average of a column of values.

Background Information

There is one input table, called Sample, that contains the following data:

Output 6.1 Sample Input Table for Weighted Averages

```
              Sample Data for Weighted Average

         Obs      Value      Weight     Gender

           1    2893.35      9.0868       F
           2      56.13     26.2171       M
           3     901.43     -4.0605       F
           4    2942.68     -5.6557       M
           5     621.16     24.3306       F
           6     361.50     13.8971       M
           7    2575.09     29.3734       F
           8    2157.07      7.0687       M
           9     690.73    -40.1271       F
          10    2085.80     24.4795       M
```

Note that some of the weights are negative.

Solution

Use the following PROC SQL code to obtain weighted averages that are shown in the following output:

```
proc sql;
   title 'Weighted Averages from Sample Data';
   select Gender, sum(Value*Weight)/sum(Weight) as WeightedAverage
      from (select Gender, Value,
                 case
                    when Weight gt 0 then Weight
                    else 0
                 end as Weight
             from Sample)
      group by Gender;
```

Output 6.2 PROC SQL Output for Weighted Averages

```
              Weighted Averages from Sample Data

                             Weighted
                  Gender      Average
                  -------------------
                    F        1864.026
                    M        1015.91
```

How It Works

This solution uses an in-line view to create a temporary table that eliminates the negative data values in the Weight column. The in-line view is a query that

☐ selects the Gender and Value columns.

□ uses a CASE expression to select the value from the Weight column. If Weight is greater than zero, then it is retrieved; if Weight is less than zero, then a value of zero is used in place of the Weight value.

```
(select Gender, Value,
        case
            when Weight>0 then Weight
            else 0
        end as Weight
    from Sample)
```

The first, or outer, SELECT statement in the query

□ selects the Gender column

□ constructs a weighted average from the results that were retrieved by the in-line view.

The weighted average is the sum of the products of Value and Weight divided by the sum of the Weights.

```
select Gender, sum(Value*Weight)/sum(Weight) as WeightedAverage
```

Finally, the query uses a GROUP BY clause to combine the data so that the calculation is performed for each gender.

```
group by Gender;
```

Comparing Tables

Problem

You have two copies of a table. One of the copies has been updated. You want to see which rows have been changed.

Background Information

There are two tables, the OLDSTAFF table and NEWSTAFF table. The NEWSTAFF table is a copy of OLDSTAFF. Changes have been made to NEWSTAFF. You want to find out what changes have been made.

Output 6.3 Sample Input Tables for Table Comparison

```
                        Old Staff Table

        id      Last        First      Middle    Phone       Location
        -------------------------------------------------------------
        5463    Olsen       Mary       K.        661-0012    R2342
        6574    Hogan       Terence    H.        661-3243    R4456
        7896    Bridges     Georgina   W.        661-8897    S2988
        4352    Anson       Sanford              661-4432    S3412
        5674    Leach       Archie     G.        661-4328    S3533
        7902    Wilson      Fran       R.        661-8332    R4454
        0001    Singleton   Adam       O.        661-0980    R4457
        9786    Thompson    Jack                 661-6781    R2343
```

```
                         New Staff Table

      id        Last        First      Middle    Phone      Location
      -----------------------------------------------------------------
      5463      Olsen       Mary       K.        661-0012   R2342
      6574      Hogan       Terence    H.        661-3243   R4456
      7896      Bridges     Georgina   W.        661-2231   S2987
      4352      Anson       Sanford              661-4432   S3412
      5674      Leach       Archie     G.        661-4328   S3533
      7902      Wilson      Fran       R.        661-8332   R4454
      0001      Singleton   Adam       O.        661-0980   R4457
      9786      Thompson    John       C.        661-6781   R2343
      2123      Chen        Bill       W.        661-8099   R4432
```

Solution

To display only the rows that have changed in the new version of the table, use the EXCEPT set operator between two SELECT statements.

```
proc sql;
   title 'Updated Rows';
   select * from newstaff
   except
   select * from oldstaff;
```

Output 6.4 Rows That Have Changed

```
                           Updated Rows

      id        Last        First      Middle    Phone      Location
      -----------------------------------------------------------------
      2123      Chen        Bill       W.        661-8099   R4432
      7896      Bridges     Georgina   W.        661-2231   S2987
      9786      Thompson    John       C.        661-6781   R2343
```

How It Works

The EXCEPT operator returns rows from the first query that are not part of the second query. In this example, the EXCEPT operator displays only the rows that have been added or changed in the NEWSTAFF table.

Note: Any rows that were deleted from OLDSTAFF will not appear. △

Overlaying Missing Data Values

Problem

You are forming teams for a new league by analyzing the averages of bowlers when they were members of other bowling leagues. When possible you will use each bowler's most recent league average. However, if a bowler was not in a league last year, then you will use the bowler's average from the prior year.

Background Information

There are two tables, LEAGUE1 and LEAGUE2, that contain bowling averages for last year and the prior year respectively. The structure of the tables is not identical because the data was compiled by two different secretaries. However, the tables do contain essentially the same type of data.

Output 6.5   Sample Input Tables for Overlaying Missing Values

```
                   Bowling Averages from League1

             Fullname              Bowler  AvgScore
             ------------------------------------
             Alexander Delarge      4224       164
             John T Chance          4425        .
             Jack T Colton          4264        .
                                    1412       141
             Andrew Shepherd        4189       185
```

```
                   Bowling Averages from League2

          FirstName   LastName       AMFNo  AvgScore
          ------------------------------------------
          Alex        Delarge         4224       156
          Mickey      Raymond         1412        .
                                      4264       174
          Jack        Chance          4425        .
          Patrick     O'Malley        4118       164
```

Solution

The following PROC SQL code combines the information from two tables, LEAGUE1 and LEAGUE2. The program uses all the values from the LEAGUE1 table, if available, and replaces any missing values with the corresponding values from the LEAGUE2 table. The results are shown in the following output.

```
options nodate nonumber linesize=80 pagesize=60;

proc sql;
```

```
title "Averages from Last Year's League When Possible";
title2 "Supplemented when Available from Prior Year's League";
select coalesce(lastyr.fullname,trim(prioryr.firstname)
            ||' '||prioryr.lastname)as Name format=$26.,
      coalesce(lastyr.bowler,prioryr.amfno)as Bowler,
      coalesce(lastyr.avgscore,prioryr.avgscore)as Average format=8.
   from league1 as lastyr full join league2 as prioryr
       on lastyr.bowler=prioryr.amfno
   order by Bowler;
```

Output 6.6 PROC SQL Output for Overlaying Missing Values

```
             Averages from Last Year's League When Possible
             Supplemented when Available from Prior Year's League

            Name                       Bowler   Average
            ------------------------------------------------
            Mickey Raymond             1412        141
            Patrick O'Malley           4118        164
            Andrew Shepherd            4189        185
            Alexander Delarge          4224        164
            Jack T Colton              4264        174
            John T Chance              4425          .
```

How It Works

This solution uses a full join to obtain all rows from LEAGUE1 as well as all rows from LEAGUE2. The program uses the COALESCE function on each column so that, whenever possible, there is a value for each column of a row. Using the COALESCE function on a list of expressions that is enclosed in parentheses returns the first nonmissing value that is found. For each row, the following code returns the AvgScore column from LEAGUE1 for Average:

```
coalesce(lastyr.avgscore,prioryr.avgscore) as Average format=8.
```

If this value of AvgScore is missing, then COALESCE returns the AvgScore column from LEAGUE2 for Average. If this value of AvgScore is missing, then COALESCE returns a missing value for Average.

In the case of the Name column, the COALESCE function returns the value of FullName from LEAGUE1 if it exists. If not, then the value is obtained from LEAGUE2 by using both the TRIM function and concatenation operators to combine the first name and last name columns:

```
trim(prioryr.firstname)||' '||prioryr.lastname
```

Finally, the table is ordered by Bowler. The Bowler column is the result of the COALESCE function.

```
coalesce(lastyr.bowler,prioryr.amfno)as Bowler
```

Because the value is obtained from either table, you cannot confidently order the output by either the value of Bowler in LEAGUE1 or the value of AMFNo in LEAGUE 2, but only by the value that results from the COALESCE function.

Computing Percentages within Subtotals

Problem

You want to analyze answers to a survey question to determine how each state responded. Then you want to compute the percentage of each answer that a given state contributed. For example, what percentage of all NO responses came from North Carolina?

Background Information

There is one input table, called SURVEY, that contains the following data (the first ten rows are shown):

Output 6.7   Input Table for Computing Subtotal Percentages (Partial Output)

```
                 Sample Data for Subtotal Percentages

                    Obs    State    Answer

                     1      NY      YES
                     2      NY      YES
                     3      NY      YES
                     4      NY      YES
                     5      NY      YES
                     6      NY      YES
                     7      NY      NO
                     8      NY      NO
                     9      NY      NO
                    10      NC      YES
```

Solution

Use the following PROC SQL code to compute the subtotal percentages:

```
proc sql;
   title1 'Survey Responses';
   select survey.Answer, State, count(State) as Count,
          calculated Count/Subtotal as Percent format=percent8.2
   from survey,
        (select Answer, count(*) as Subtotal from survey
            group by Answer) as survey2
   where survey.Answer=survey2.Answer
   group by survey.Answer, State;
quit;
```

Output 6.8 PROC SQL Output That Computes Percentages within Subtotals

```
                     Survey Responses

        Answer    State      Count    Percent
        ----------------------------------------
        NO        NC            24    38.71%
        NO        NY             3     4.84%
        NO        PA            18    29.03%
        NO        VA            17    27.42%
        YES       NC            20    37.04%
        YES       NY             6    11.11%
        YES       PA             9    16.67%
        YES       VA            19    35.19%
```

How It Works

This solution uses a subquery to calculate the subtotal counts for each answer. The code joins the result of the subquery with the original table and then uses the calculated state count as the numerator and the subtotal from the subquery as the denominator for the percentage calculation.

The query uses a GROUP BY clause to combine the data so that the calculation is performed for State within each answer.

```
group by survey.Answer, State;
```

Counting Duplicate Rows in a Table

Problem

You want to count the number of duplicate rows in a table and generate an output column that shows how many times each row occurs.

Background Information

There is one input table, called DUPLICATES, that contains the following data:

Output 6.9   Sample Input Table for Counting Duplicates

```
                   Sample Data for Counting Duplicates

                          First
          Obs   LastName   Name        City        State

           1    Smith      John        Richmond    Virginia
           2    Johnson    Mary        Miami       Florida
           3    Smith      John        Richmond    Virginia
           4    Reed       Sam         Portland    Oregon
           5    Davis      Karen       Chicago     Illinois
           6    Davis      Karen       Chicago     Illinois
           7    Thompson   Jennifer    Houston     Texas
           8    Smith      John        Richmond    Virginia
           9    Johnson    Mary        Miami       Florida
```

Solution

Use the following PROC SQL code to count the duplicate rows:

```
proc sql;
   title 'Duplicate Rows in DUPLICATES Table';
   select *, count(*) as Count
      from Duplicates
      group by LastName, FirstName, City, State
      having count(*) > 1;
```

Output 6.10   PROC SQL Output for Counting Duplicates

```
                   Duplicate Rows in DUPLICATES Table

          LastName   FirstName  City       State       Count
          ---------------------------------------------------
          Davis      Karen      Chicago    Illinois      2
          Johnson    Mary       Miami      Florida       2
          Smith      John       Richmond   Virginia      3
```

How It Works

This solution uses a query that
- selects all columns
- counts all rows
- groups all of the rows in the Duplicates table by matching rows
- excludes the rows that have no duplicates.

Note: You must include all of the columns in your table in the GROUP BY clause to find exact duplicates. △

Expanding Hierarchical Data in a Table

Problem

You want to generate an output column that shows a hierarchical relationship among rows in a table.

Background Information

There is one input table, called EMPLOYEES, that contains the following data:

Output 6.11 Sample Input Table for Expanding a Hierarchy

```
                Sample Data for Expanding a Hierarchy

                                     First
            Obs     ID    LastName   Name        Supervisor

             1     1001   Smith      John           1002
             2     1002   Johnson    Mary           None
             3     1003   Reed       Sam            None
             4     1004   Davis      Karen          1003
             5     1005   Thompson   Jennifer       1002
             6     1006   Peterson   George         1002
             7     1007   Jones      Sue            1003
             8     1008   Murphy     Janice         1003
             9     1009   Garcia     Joe            1002
```

You want to create output that shows the full name and ID number of each employee who has a supervisor, along with the full name and ID number of that employee's supervisor.

Solution

Use the following PROC SQL code to expand the data:

```
proc sql;
   title 'Expanded Employee and Supervisor Data';
   select A.ID label="Employee ID",
          trim(A.FirstName)||' '||A.LastName label="Employee Name",
          B.ID label="Supervisor ID",
          trim(B.FirstName)||' '||B.LastName label="Supervisor Name"
      from Employees A, Employees B
      where A.Supervisor=B.ID and A.Supervisor is not missing;
```

Output 6.12 PROC SQL Output for Expanding a Hierarchy

```
                    Expanded Employee and Supervisor Data

          Employee                        Supervisor
          ID        Employee Name         ID        Supervisor Name
          ------------------------------------------------------------
          1001      John Smith            1002      Mary Johnson
          1005      Jennifer Thompson     1002      Mary Johnson
          1006      George Peterson       1002      Mary Johnson
          1009      Joe Garcia            1002      Mary Johnson
          1004      Karen Davis           1003      Sam Reed
          1007      Sue Jones             1003      Sam Reed
          1008      Janice Murphy         1003      Sam Reed
```

How It Works

This solution uses a self-join (reflexive join) to match employees and their supervisors. The SELECT clause assigns aliases of A and B to two instances of the same table and retrieves data from each instance. From instance A, the SELECT clause

- □ selects the ID column and assigns it a label of **Employee ID**
- □ selects and concatenates the FirstName and LastName columns into one output column and assigns it a label of **Employee Name**.

From instance B, the SELECT clause

- □ selects the ID column and assigns it a label of **Supervisor ID**
- □ selects and concatenates the FirstName and LastName columns into one output column and assigns it a label of **Supervisor Name**.

In both concatenations, the SELECT clause uses the TRIM function to remove trailing spaces from the data in the FirstName column, and then concatenates the data with a single space and the data in the LastName column to produce a single character value for each full name.

```
trim(A.FirstName)||' '||A.LastName label="Employee Name"
```

When PROC SQL applies the WHERE clause, the two table instances are joined. The WHERE clause conditions restrict the output to only those rows in table A that have a supervisor ID that matches an employee ID in table B. This operation provides a supervisor ID and full name for each employee in the original table, except for those who do not have a supervisor.

```
where A.Supervisor=B.ID and A.Supervisor is not missing;
```

Note: Although there are no missing values in the Employees table, you should check for and exclude missing values from your results to avoid unexpected results. For example, if there were an employee with a blank supervisor ID number and an employee with a blank ID, then they would produce an erroneous match in the results. △

Summarizing Data in Multiple Columns

Problem

You want to produce a grand total of multiple columns in a table.

Background Information

There is one input table, called SALES, that contains the following data:

Output 6.13 Sample Input Table for Summarizing Data from Multiple Columns

```
        Sample Data for Summarizing Data from Multiple Columns

        Obs     Salesperson     January     February     March

         1      Smith            1000          650         800
         2      Johnson             0          900         900
         3      Reed             1200          700         850
         4      Davis            1050          900        1000
         5      Thompson          750          850        1000
         6      Peterson          900          600         500
         7      Jones             800          900        1200
         8      Murphy            700          800         700
         9      Garcia            400         1200        1150
```

You want to create output that shows the total sales for each month and the total sales for all three months.

Solution

Use the following PROC SQL code to produce the monthly totals and grand total:

```
proc sql;
   title 'Total First Quarter Sales';
   select sum(January)  as JanTotal,
          sum(February) as FebTotal,
          sum(March)    as MarTotal,
          sum(calculated JanTotal, calculated FebTotal,
              calculated MarTotal) as GrandTotal format=dollar10.
      from Sales;
```

Output 6.14   PROC SQL Output for Summarizing Data from Multiple Columns

```
                       Total First Quarter Sales

            JanTotal  FebTotal  MarTotal  GrandTotal
            ------------------------------------------
                6800      7500      8100    $22,400
```

How It Works

Recall that when you specify one column as the argument to an aggregate function, the values in that column are calculated. When you specify multiple columns, the values in each row of the columns are calculated. This solution uses the SUM function to calculate the sum of each month's sales, and then uses the SUM function a second time to total the monthly sums into one grand total.

```
sum(calculated JanTotal, calculated FebTotal,
    calculated MarTotal) as GrandTotal format=dollar10.
```

An alternative way to code the grand total calculation is to use nested functions:

```
sum(sum(January), sum(February), sum(March))
   as GrandTotal format=dollar10.
```

Creating a Summary Report

Problem

You have a table that contains detailed sales information. You want to produce a summary report from the detail table.

Background Information

There is one input table, called SALES, that contains detailed sales information. There is one record for each sale for the first quarter that shows the site, product, invoice number, invoice amount, and invoice date.

Output 6.15 Sample Input Table for Creating a Summary Report

```
           Sample Data to Create Summary Sales Report

                                    Invoice
         Site    Product   Invoice   Amount  InvoiceDate
         ----------------------------------------------------
         V1009   VID010    V7679      598.5  980126
         V1019   VID010    V7688      598.5  980126
         V1032   VID005    V7771       1070  980309
         V1043   VID014    V7780       1070  980309
         V421    VID003    V7831       2000  980330
         V421    VID010    V7832        750  980330
         V570    VID003    V7762       2000  980302
         V659    VID003    V7730       1000  980223
         V783    VID003    V7815        750  980323
         V985    VID003    V7733       2500  980223
         V966    VID001    V5020       1167  980215
         V98     VID003    V7750       2000  980223
```

You want to use this table to create a summary report that shows the sales for each product for each month of the quarter.

Solution

Use the following PROC SQL code to create a column for each month of the quarter, and use the summary function SUM in combination with the GROUP BY statement to accumulate the monthly sales for each product:

```
proc sql;
   title 'First Quarter Sales by Product';
   select Product,
          sum(Jan) label='Jan',
          sum(Feb) label='Feb',
          sum(Mar) label='Mar'
      from (select Product,
                   case
                      when substr(InvoiceDate,3,2)='01' then
                         InvoiceAmount end as Jan,
                   case
                      when substr(InvoiceDate,3,2)='02' then
                         InvoiceAmount end as Feb,
                   case
                      when substr(InvoiceDate,3,2)='03' then
                         InvoiceAmount end as Mar
               from work.sales)
      group by Product;
```

Output 6.16   PROC SQL Output for a Summary Report

```
                    First Quarter Sales by Product


             Product        Jan        Feb        Mar
             ---------------------------------------------
             VID001           .        1167          .
             VID003           .        5500        4750
             VID005           .           .        1070
             VID010         1197          .         750
             VID014           .           .        1070
```

Note: Missing values in the matrix indicate that no sales occurred for that given product in that month. △

How It Works

This solution uses an in-line view to create three temporary columns, Jan, Feb, and Mar, based on the month part of the invoice date column. The in-line view is a query that

□   selects the product column

□   uses a CASE expression to assign the value of invoice amount to one of three columns, Jan, Feb, or Mar, depending upon the value of the month part of the invoice date column.

```
case
    when substr(InvoiceDate,3,2)='01' then
        InvoiceAmount end as Jan,
    case
        when substr(InvoiceSate,3,2)='02' then
            InvoiceAmount end as Feb,
    case
        when substr(InvoiceDate,3,2)='03' then
            InvoiceAmount end as Mar
```

The first, or outer, SELECT statement in the query

□   selects the product

□   uses the summary function SUM to accumulate the Jan, Feb, and Mar amounts

□   uses the GROUP BY statement to produce a line in the table for each product.

Notice that dates are stored in the input table as strings. If the dates were stored as SAS dates, then the CASE expression could be written as follows:

```
case
    when month(InvoiceDate)=1 then
        InvoiceAmount end as Jan,
case
    when month(InvoiceDate)=2 then
        InvoiceAmount end as Feb,
case
    when month(InvoiceDate)=3 then
        InvoiceAmount end as Mar
```

Creating a Customized Sort Order

Problem

You want to sort data in a logical, but not alphabetical, sequence.

Background Information

There is one input table, called CHORES, that contains the following data:

Output 6.17 Sample Input Data for a Customized Sort

```
                          Garden Chores

                  Project      Hours  Season
                  ---------------------------
                  weeding        48   summer
                  pruning        12   winter
                  mowing         36   summer
                  mulching       17   fall
                  raking         24   fall
                  raking         16   spring
                  planting        8   spring
                  planting        8   fall
                  sweeping        3   winter
                  edging         16   summer
                  seeding         6   spring
                  tilling        12   spring
                  aerating        6   spring
                  feeding         7   summer
                  rolling         4   winter
```

You want to reorder this chore list so that all the chores are grouped by season, starting with spring and progressing through the year. Simply ordering by Season makes the list appear in alphabetical sequence: fall, spring, summer, winter.

Solution

Use the following PROC SQL code to create a new column, Sorter, that will have values of 1 through 4 for the seasons spring through winter. Use the new column to order the query, but do not select it to appear:

```
options nodate nonumber linesize=80 pagesize=60;

 proc sql;
    title 'Garden Chores by Season in Logical Order';
    select Project, Hours, Season
       from (select Project, Hours, Season,
                case
                    when Season = 'spring' then 1
                    when Season = 'summer' then 2
```

```
                when Season = 'fall' then 3
                when Season = 'winter' then 4
                else .
            end as Sorter
        from chores)
    order by Sorter;
```

Output 6.18 PROC SQL Output for a Customized Sort Sequence

```
                Garden Chores by Season in Logical Order

                    Project      Hours  Season
                    ---------------------------
                    tilling         12  spring
                    raking          16  spring
                    planting         8  spring
                    seeding          6  spring
                    aerating         6  spring
                    mowing          36  summer
                    feeding          7  summer
                    edging          16  summer
                    weeding         48  summer
                    raking          24  fall
                    mulching        17  fall
                    planting         8  fall
                    rolling          4  winter
                    pruning         12  winter
                    sweeping         3  winter
```

How It Works

This solution uses an in-line view to create a temporary column that can be used as an ORDER BY column. The in-line view is a query that

  □ selects the Project, Hours, and Season columns

  □ uses a CASE expression to remap the seasons to the new column Sorter: spring to 1, summer to 2, fall to 3, and winter to 4.

```
    (select project, hours, season,
        case
            when season = 'spring' then 1
            when season = 'summer' then 2
            when season = 'fall' then 3
            when season = 'winter' then 4
            else .
        end as sorter
    from chores)
```

The first, or outer, SELECT statement in the query

  □ selects the Project, Hours and Season columns

  □ orders rows by the values that were assigned to the seasons in the Sorter column that was created with the in-line view.

Notice that the Sorter column is not included in the SELECT statement. That causes a note to be written to the log indicating that you have used a column in an ORDER BY statement that does not appear in the SELECT statement. In this case, that is exactly what you wanted to do.

Conditionally Updating a Table

Problem

You want to update values in a column of a table, based on the values of several other columns in the table.

Background Information

There is one table, called INCENTIVES, that contains information on sales data. There is one record for each salesperson that includes a department code, a base pay rate, and sales of two products, gadgets and whatnots.

Output 6.19   Sample Input Data to Conditionally Change a Table

```
                   Sales Data for Incentives Program

        Name              Department  Payrate  Gadgets  Whatnots
        ---------------------------------------------------------
        Lao Che           M2               8    10193      1105
        Jack Colton       U2               6     9994      2710
        Mickey Raymond    M1              12     6103      1930
        Dean Proffit      M2              11     3000      1999
        Antoinette Lily   E1              20     2203      4610
        Sydney Wade       E2              15     4205      3010
        Alan Traherne     U2               4     5020      3000
        Elizabeth Bennett E1              16    17003      3003
```

You want to update the table by increasing each salesperson's payrate (based on the total sales of gadgets and whatnots) and taking into consideration some factors that are based on department code.

Specifically, anyone who sells over 10,000 gadgets merits an extra $5 per hour. Anyone selling between 5,000 and 10,000 gadgets also merits an incentive pay, but E Department salespersons are expected to be better sellers than those in the other departments, so their gadget sales incentive is $2 per hour compared to $3 per hour for those in other departments. Good sales of whatnots also entitle sellers to added incentive pay. The algorithm for whatnot sales is that the top level (level 1 in each department) salespersons merit an extra $.50 per hour for whatnot sales over 2,000, and level 2 salespersons merit an extra $1 per hour for sales over 2,000.

Solution

Use the following PROC SQL code to create a new value for the Payrate column. Actually Payrate is updated twice for each row, once based on sales of gadgets, and again based on sales of whatnots:

```
proc sql;
   update incentives
   set payrate = case
```

```
               when gadgets > 10000 then
                   payrate + 5.00
               when gadgets > 5000 then
                   case
                       when department in ('E1', 'E2') then
                           payrate + 2.00
                       else payrate + 3.00
                   end
               else payrate
           end;
update incentives
set payrate = case
                when whatnots > 2000 then
                    case
                        when department in ('E2', 'M2', 'U2') then
                            payrate + 1.00
                        else payrate + 0.50
                    end
                else payrate
            end;
title 'Adjusted Payrates Based on Sales of Gadgets and Whatnots';
select * from incentives;
```

Output 6.20   PROC SQL Output for Conditionally Updating a Table

```
        Adjusted Payrates Based on Sales of Gadgets and Whatnots

    Name                Department   Payrate   Gadgets   Whatnots
    -------------------------------------------------------------------
    Lao Che             M2                13     10193       1105
    Jack Colton         U2                10      9994       2710
    Mickey Raymond      M1                15      6103       1930
    Dean Proffit        M2                11      3000       1999
    Antoinette Lily     E1              20.5      2203       4610
    Sydney Wade         E2                16      4205       3010
    Alan Traherne       U2                 8      5020       3000
    Elizabeth Bennett   E1              21.5     17003       3003
```

How It Works

This solution performs consecutive updates to the payrate column of the incentive table. The first update uses a nested case expression, first determining a bracket that is based on the amount of gadget sales: greater than 10,000 calls for an incentive of $5, between 5,000 and 10,000 requires an additional comparison. That is accomplished with a nested case expression that checks department code to choose between a $2 and $3 incentive.

```
update incentives
set payrate = case
                when gadgets > 10000 then
                    payrate + 5.00
                when gadgets > 5000 then
                    case
```

```
                    when department in ('E1', 'E2') then
                        payrate + 2.00
                    else payrate + 3.00
                end
            else payrate
        end;
```

The second update is similar, though simpler. All sales of whatnots over 2,000 merit an incentive, either $.50 or $1 depending on the department level, that again is accomplished by means of a nested case expression.

```
update incentives
   set payrate = case
                    when whatnots > 2000 then
                        case
                            when department in ('E2', 'M2', 'U2') then
                                payrate + 1.00
                            else payrate + 0.50
                        end
                    else payrate
                end;
```

Updating a Table with Values from Another Table

Problem

You want to update the SQL.UNITEDSTATES table with updated population data.

Background Information

The SQL.NEWPOP table contains updated population data for some of the U.S. states.

Output 6.21   Table with Updated Population Data

```
                         Updated U.S. Population Data

                 state                        Population
                 -----------------------------------------------
                 Texas                         20,851,820
                 Georgia                        8,186,453
                 Washington                     5,894,121
                 Arizona                        5,130,632
                 Alabama                        4,447,100
                 Oklahoma                       3,450,654
                 Connecticut                    3,405,565
                 Iowa                           2,926,324
                 West Virginia                  1,808,344
                 Idaho                          1,293,953
                 Maine                          1,274,923
                 New Hampshire                  1,235,786
                 North Dakota                      642,200
                 Alaska                            626,932
```

Solution

Use the following PROC SQL code to update the population information for each state in the SQL.UNITEDSTATES table:

```
proc sql;
title 'UNITEDSTATES';
update sql.unitedstates as u
   set population=(select population from sql.newpop as n
   where u.name=n.state)
  where u.name in (select state from sql.newpop);
select Name format=$17., Capital format=$15.,
      Population, Area, Continent format=$13., Statehood format=date9.
   from sql.unitedstates;
```

Output 6.22   SQL.UNITEDSTATES with Updated Population Data (Partial Output)

```
                                      UNITEDSTATES

Name               Capital          Population      Area  Continent        Statehood
-------------------------------------------------------------------------------------
Alabama            Montgomery          4447100     52423  North America    14DEC1819
Alaska             Juneau               626932    656400  North America    03JAN1959
Arizona            Phoenix             5130632    114000  North America    14FEB1912
Arkansas           Little Rock         2447996     53200  North America    15JUN1836
California         Sacramento         31518948    163700  North America    09SEP1850
Colorado           Denver              3601298    104100  North America    01AUG1876
Connecticut        Hartford            3405565      5500  North America    09JAN1788
Delaware           Dover                707232      2500  North America    07DEC1787
District of Colum  Washington           612907       100  North America    21FEB1871
Florida            Tallahassee        13814408     65800  North America    03MAR1845
```

How It Works

The UPDATE statement updates values in the SQL.UNITEDSTATES table (here with the alias U). For each row in the SQL.UNITEDSTATES table, the in-line view in the SET clause returns a single value. For rows that have a corresponding row in SQL.NEWPOP, this value is the value of the Population column from SQL.NEWPOP. For rows that do not have a corresponding row in SQL.NEWPOP, this value is missing. In both cases, the returned value is assigned to the Population column.

The WHERE clause ensures that only the rows in SQL.UNITEDSTATES that have a corresponding row in SQL.NEWPOP are updated, by checking each value of Name against the list of state names that is returned from the in-line view. Without the WHERE clause, rows that do not have a corresponding row in SQL.NEWPOP would have their Population values updated to missing.

Creating and Using Macro Variables

Problem

You want to create a separate data set for each unique value of a column.

Background Information

The SQL.FEATURES data set contains information on various geographical features around the world.

Output 6.23 FEATURES (Partial Output)

```
                                      FEATURES

  Name            Type        Location          Area    Height    Depth    Length
  ------------------------------------------------------------------------------------
  Aconcagua       Mountain    Argentina            .     22834        .         .
  Amazon          River       South America        .         .        .      4000
  Amur            River       Asia                 .         .        .      2700
  Andaman         Sea                         218100         .     3667         .
  Angel Falls     Waterfall   Venezuela            .      3212        .         .
  Annapurna       Mountain    Nepal                .     26504        .         .
  Aral Sea        Lake        Asia             25300         .      222         .
  Ararat          Mountain    Turkey               .     16804        .         .
  Arctic          Ocean                      5105700         .    17880         .
  Atlantic        Ocean                     33420000         .    28374         .
```

Solution

To create a separate data set for each type of feature, you could go through the data set manually to determine all the unique values of Type, and then write a separate DATA step for each type (or a single DATA step with multiple OUTPUT statements).

This approach is labor-intensive, error-prone, and impractical for large data sets. The following PROC SQL code counts the unique values of Type and puts each value in a separate macro variable. The SAS macro that follows the PROC SQL code uses these macro variables to create a SAS data set for each value. You do not need to know beforehand how many unique values there are or what the values are.

```
proc sql noprint;
   select count(distinct type)
      into :n
      from sql.features;
   select distinct type
      into :type1 - :type%left(&n)
      from sql.features;
quit;

%macro makeds;
   %do i=1 %to &n;
      data &&type&i (drop=type);
         set sql.features;
         if type="&&type&i";
      run;
   %end;
%mend makeds;
%makeds;
```

Output 6.24 Log

```
240  proc sql noprint;
241     select count(distinct type)
242        into :n
243        from sql.features;
244     select distinct type
245        into :type1 - :type%left(&n)
246        from sql.features;
247  quit;
NOTE: PROCEDURE SQL used (Total process time):
      real time            0.04 seconds
      cpu time             0.03 seconds


248
249  %macro makeds;
250     %do i=1 %to &n;
251        data &&type&i (drop=type);
252           set sql.features;
253           if type="&&type&i";
254        run;
255     %end;
256  %mend makeds;
257  %makeds;
NOTE: There were 74 observations read from the data set SQL.FEATURES.
NOTE: The data set WORK.DESERT has 7 observations and 6 variables.
NOTE: DATA statement used (Total process time):
      real time            1.14 seconds
      cpu time             0.41 seconds


NOTE: There were 74 observations read from the data set SQL.FEATURES.
NOTE: The data set WORK.ISLAND has 6 observations and 6 variables.
NOTE: DATA statement used (Total process time):
      real time            0.02 seconds
      cpu time             0.00 seconds


NOTE: There were 74 observations read from the data set SQL.FEATURES.
NOTE: The data set WORK.LAKE has 10 observations and 6 variables.
NOTE: DATA statement used (Total process time):
      real time            0.01 seconds
      cpu time             0.01 seconds


NOTE: There were 74 observations read from the data set SQL.FEATURES.
NOTE: The data set WORK.MOUNTAIN has 18 observations and 6 variables.
NOTE: DATA statement used (Total process time):
      real time            0.02 seconds
      cpu time             0.01 seconds


NOTE: There were 74 observations read from the data set SQL.FEATURES.
NOTE: The data set WORK.OCEAN has 4 observations and 6 variables.
NOTE: DATA statement used (Total process time):
      real time            0.01 seconds
      cpu time             0.01 seconds


NOTE: There were 74 observations read from the data set SQL.FEATURES.
NOTE: The data set WORK.RIVER has 12 observations and 6 variables.
NOTE: DATA statement used (Total process time):
      real time            0.02 seconds
      cpu time             0.02 seconds


NOTE: There were 74 observations read from the data set SQL.FEATURES.
NOTE: The data set WORK.SEA has 13 observations and 6 variables.
NOTE: DATA statement used (Total process time):
      real time            0.03 seconds
      cpu time             0.02 seconds


NOTE: There were 74 observations read from the data set SQL.FEATURES.
NOTE: The data set WORK.WATERFALL has 4 observations and 6 variables.
NOTE: DATA statement used (Total process time):
      real time            0.02 seconds
      cpu time             0.02 seconds
```

How It Works

This solution uses the INTO clause to store values in macro variables. The first SELECT statement counts the unique variables and stores the result in macro variable N. The second SELECT statement creates a range of macro variables, one for each unique value, and stores each unique value in one of the macro variables. Note the use of the %LEFT function, which trims leading blanks from the value of the N macro variable.

The MAKEDS macro uses all the macro variables that were created in the PROC SQL step. The macro uses a %DO loop to execute a DATA step for each unique value, writing rows that contain a given value of Type to a SAS data set of the same name. The Type variable is dropped from the output data sets.

For more information about SAS macros, see *SAS Macro Language: Reference*.

Using PROC SQL Tables in Other SAS Procedures

Problem

You want to show the average high temperatures in degrees Celsius for European countries on a map.

Background Information

The SQL.WORLDTEMPS table has average high and low temperatures for various cities around the world.

Output 6.25   WORLDTEMPS (Partial Output)

```
                          WORLDTEMPS

       City            Country         AvgHigh    AvgLow
       ----------------------------------------------------
       Algiers         Algeria            90         45
       Amsterdam       Netherlands        70         33
       Athens          Greece             89         41
       Auckland        New Zealand        75         44
       Bangkok         Thailand           95         69
       Beijing         China              86         17
       Belgrade        Yugoslavia         80         29
       Berlin          Germany            75         25
       Bogota          Colombia           69         43
       Bombay          India              90         68
```

Solution

Use the following PROC SQL and PROC GMAP code to produce the map. You must license SAS/GRAPH software to use PROC GMAP.

```
options fmtsearch=(sashelp.mapfmts);

proc sql;
   create table extremetemps as
   select country, round((mean(avgHigh)-32)/1.8) as High,
      input(put(country,$glcsmn.), best.) as ID
   from sql.worldtemps
   where calculated id is not missing and country in
      (select name from sql.countries where continent='Europe')
   group by country;
quit;

proc gmap map=maps.europe data=extremetemps all;
   id id;
   block high / levels=3;
   title 'Average High Temperatures for European Countries';
   title2 'Degrees Celsius'
run;
quit;
```

Figure 6.1   PROC GMAP Output

Average High Temperatures for European Countries
Degrees Celsius

High   20 - 23   24 - 26   27 - 32

How It Works

The SAS system option FMTSEARCH= tells SAS to search in the SASHELP.MAPFMTS catalog for map-related formats. In the PROC SQL step, a temporary table is created with Country, High, and ID columns. The calculation `round((mean(avgHigh)-32)/1.8)` does the following:

1 For countries that are represented by more than one city, the mean of the cities' average high temperatures is used for that country.

2 That value is converted from degrees Fahrenheit to degrees Celsius.

3 The result is rounded to the nearest degree.

The PUT function uses the $GLCSMN. format to convert the country name to a country code. The INPUT function converts this country code, which is returned by the PUT function as a character value, into a numeric value that can be understood by the GMAP procedure. See *SAS Language Reference: Dictionary* for details about the PUT and INPUT functions.

The WHERE clause limits the output to European countries by checking the value of the Country column against the list of European countries that is returned by the in-line view. Also, rows with missing values of ID are eliminated. Missing ID values could be produced if the $GLCSMN. format does not recognize the country name.

The GROUP BY clause is required so that the mean temperature can be calculated for each country rather than for the entire table.

The PROC GMAP step uses the ID variable to identify each country and places a block representing the High value on each country on the map. The ALL option ensures that countries (such as the United Kingdom in this example) that do not have High values are also drawn on the map. In the BLOCK statement, the LEVELS= option specifies how many response levels are used in the graph. For more information about the GMAP procedure, see *SAS/GRAPH: Reference*.

APPENDIX

1

Recommended Reading

Recommended Reading

Here is the recommended reading list for this title:

- □ *Base SAS Procedures Guide*
- □ *Cody's Data Cleaning Techniques Using SAS Software*
- □ *Combining and Modifying SAS Data Sets: Examples*
- □ *SAS/GRAPH: Reference*
- □ *SAS Language Reference: Concepts*
- □ *SAS Language Reference: Dictionary*
- □ *SAS Macro Language: Reference*

For a complete list of SAS publications, go to **support.sas.com/bookstore**. If you have questions about which titles you need, please contact a SAS Publishing Sales Representative at:

SAS Publishing Sales
SAS Campus Drive
Cary, NC 27513
Telephone: 1-800-727-3228
Fax: 1-919-531-9439
E-mail: **sasbook@sas.com**
Web address: **support.sas.com/bookstore**

Customers outside the United States and Canada, please contact your local SAS office for assistance.

Glossary

calculated column
in a query, a column that does not exist in any of the tables that are being queried, but which is created as a result of a column expression. See also column expression.

Cartesian product
a type of join that matches each row from each joined table to each row from all other joined tables. See also cross join and join.

column
in relational databases, a vertical component of a table. Each column has a unique name, contains data of a specific type, and has certain attributes. A column is analogous to a variable in SAS terminology.

column alias
a temporary, alternate name for a column. Aliases are optional and can be specified in the SQL procedure's SELECT clause to name or rename columns. An alias is one word. See also column.

column expression
a set of operators and operands that, when evaluated, result in a single data value. The resulting data value can be either a character value or a numeric value.

composite index
an index that locates observations in a SAS data set by examining the values of two or more key variables. See also index and simple index.

condition
in the SQL procedure, the part of the WHERE clause that contains the search criteria. In the condition, you specify which rows are to be retrieved.

cross join
a type of join that returns the product of joined tables. A cross join is functionally the same as a Cartesian product. See also Cartesian product and join.

DISTINCT
a keyword that causes the SQL procedure to remove duplicate rows from the output.

equijoin
a kind of join in the SQL procedure. For example, when two tables are joined in an equijoin, the value of a column in the first table must equal the value of the column in the second table in the SQL expression. See also join.

group

in the SQL procedure, a set of rows that all have the same combination of values for the columns that are specified in a GROUP BY clause.

index

in SAS software, a component of a SAS data set that contains the data values of a key variable or variables, paired with a location identifier for the observation that contains the value. The value/identifier pairs are ordered in a structure that enables SAS to search by a value of a variable. See also composite index and simple index.

in-line view

a query-expression that is nested in the SQL procedure's FROM clause. An in-line view produces a table internally that the outer query uses to select data. You save a programming step when you use an in-line view, because instead of creating a view and then referring to it in another query, you can specify the view in-line in the FROM clause. An in-line view can be referenced only in the query (or statement) in which it is defined. See also query-expression.

inner join

See join.

integrity constraints

a set of data validation rules that you can specify in order to restrict the data values that can be stored for a variable in a SAS data file. Integrity constraints help you preserve the validity and consistency of your data.

join

in the SQL procedure, the combination of data from two or more tables (or from two or more SAS data views) to produce a single result table. A conventional join, which is often called an inner join, returns a result table for all the rows in one table that have one or more matching rows in the other table or tables. See also outer join.

join criteria

the set of parameters that determine how tables are to be joined. Join criteria are usually specified in a WHERE expression or in an SQL ON clause. See also join and outer join.

missing value

in SAS, a term that describes the contents of a variable that contains no data for a particular row (or observation). By default, SAS prints or displays a missing numeric value as a single period, and it prints or displays a missing character value as a blank space. In the SQL procedure, a missing value is equivalent to an SQL NULL value.

natural join

a type of join that returns selected rows from tables in which one or more columns in each table have the same name and the same data type and contain the same value. See also join.

outer join

in the SQL procedure, an inner join that is augmented with rows that do not match any row from the other table or tables in the join. There are three kinds of outer joins: left, right, and full. See also join.

PROC SQL view

a SAS data set that is created by the SQL procedure. A PROC SQL view contains no data. Instead, it stores information that enables it to read data values from other files, which can include SAS data files, SAS/ACCESS views, DATA step views, or other PROC SQL views. The output of a PROC SQL view can be either a subset or a superset of one or more files. See also SAS data view.

query

a set of instructions that requests particular information from one or more data sources.

query-expression

in PROC SQL, one or more table-expressions that can be linked with set operators. The primary purpose of a query-expression is to retrieve data from tables, PROC SQL views, or SAS/ACCESS views. In PROC SQL, the SELECT statement is contained in a query-expression.

row

in relational database management systems, the horizontal component of a table. A row is analogous to a SAS observation.

SAS data file

a type of SAS data set that contains data values and descriptor information that is associated with the data. The descriptor information includes the data types and lengths of the variables as well as the name of the engine that was used to create the data. A PROC SQL table is a SAS data file. See also SAS data set and SAS data view.

SAS data set

a file whose contents are in one of the native SAS file formats. There are two types of SAS data sets: SAS data files and SAS data views. SAS data files contain data values in addition to descriptor information that is associated with the data. SAS data views contain only the descriptor information plus other information that is required for retrieving data values from other SAS data sets or from files that are stored in other software vendors' file formats.

SAS data view

a type of SAS data set that retrieves data values from other files. A SAS data view contains only descriptor information such as the data types and lengths of the variables (columns) plus other information that is required for retrieving data values from other SAS data sets or from files that are stored in other software vendors' file formats. SAS data views can be created by the SAS DATA step and by the SAS SQL procedure. See also SAS data set.

simple index

an index that uses the values of only one variable to locate observations. See also composite index and index.

SQL (Structured Query Language)

a standardized, high-level query language that is used in relational database management systems to create and manipulate objects in a database management system. SAS implements SQL through the SQL procedure.

Structured Query Language

See SQL (Structured Query Language),

table

in the SQL procedure, a SAS data file. See also SAS data file.

union join

a type of join that returns all rows with their respective values from each input table. Columns that do not exist in one table will have null (missing) values for those rows in the result table. See also join.

view

a generic term (used by many software vendors) for a definition of a virtual data set (or table). The definition is named and stored for later use. A view contains no data; it merely describes or defines data that is stored elsewhere.

WHERE clause
in the SQL procedure, the keyword WHERE followed by one or more WHERE expressions.

WHERE expression
a type of SAS expression that specifies a condition for selecting observations for processing by a DATA step or a PROC step. WHERE expressions can contain special operators that are not available in other SAS expressions. WHERE expressions can appear in a WHERE statement, a WHERE= data set option, a WHERE clause, or a WHERE command.

Index

A

abbreviating column names 58
aggregate functions 40
    creating macro variables from result of 129
    HAVING clause with 53
    table of 40
    using 40
    with unique values 44
alias
    assigning a column alias 20
    referring to calculated columns by 21
    table aliases 58
ALL keyword
    set operators and 117
automatic macro variables 128, 133
averages, weighted 146

B

BETWEEN-AND operators
    retrieving rows 36
Boolean operators
    retrieving rows 33

C

calculated columns 19
    assigning column alias to 20
    referring to by alias 21
    sorting by 28
Cartesian product 57
    cross joins 68
CASE expression
    assigning values conditionally 22
CASE-OPERAND form
    assigning values conditionally 23
COALESCE function
    in joins 70
    replacing missing values 24
column alias 20
    assigning to calculated columns 20
    referring to calculated columns 21
column attributes
    list of 17
    specifying 24
column definitions
    creating tables from 90

column headers
    suppressing 19
column names
    abbreviating 58
    qualifying 58
columns 2
    adding 99
    altering 99
    assigning values conditionally 21
    calculating values 19
    changing formats 100
    changing informats 100
    changing labels 100
    changing width 100
    creating 18
    deleting 101
    DICTIONARY.COLUMNS 125
    grouping by multiple columns 48
    grouping by one column 47
    list of, with attributes 17
    locating specific columns 125
    modifying 100
    multicolumn joins 62
    renaming 100
    replacing missing values 24
    selecting 14
    selecting all 14
    selecting specific 15
    sorting, with missing values 30
    sorting by 26
    sorting by column position 29
    sorting by multiple columns 26
    sorting by unselected columns 29
    summarizing data in multiple columns 157
    unique values 16
comparison operators
    inner joins with 59
    retrieving rows with 32
    truncated string 38
composite indexes 102
concatenating
    query results 85
    values in macro variables 130
conditional operators
    retrieving rows with 34
correlated subqueries 76
counting
    all rows 45
    duplicate rows 153
    nonmissing values 45

unique values   44
CREATE INDEX statement   102
cross joins   68

D

data files
  See tables
data set options
  creating tables with   93
  SQL procedure with   127
DATA step
  compared with SQL procedure   3
  match-merges   71
DATE function
  replacing references to   119
DATETIME function
  replacing references to   119
DBMS
  accessing with SAS/ACCESS   137
  connecting with LIBNAME statement   138
  connecting with Pass-Through Facility   140
DBMS tables   2
  PROC SQL views of   139
  querying   138
debugging queries   112
DESCRIBE VIEW statement   123
DICTIONARY tables   120
  performance and   126
  retrieving information about   122
  using   124
  views and   120
DICTIONARY.COLUMNS   125
DICTIONARY.TABLES   124

E

errors
  caused by missing values   46
  grouping errors caused by missing values   50
  update errors   98
example tables   5
EXCEPT operator
  combining queries   81, 83
execution time   114
existence of a group of values   77
EXISTS condition   77
expanded SELECT * statement   113

F

FEEDBACK option
  expanding SELECT * statement with   113
fields
  See columns
files
  See tables
filtering grouped data   51
  HAVING clause versus WHERE clause   52
  using a simple HAVING clause   51
  using HAVING clause with aggregate functions   53
foreign key   104
formats
  changing column format   100
  deploying inside Teradata   119
FROM clause   12

full outer joins   67

G

general integrity constraints   104
GROUP BY clause   13
grouping data   47
  by multiple columns   48
  by one column   47
  filtering grouped data   51
  finding errors caused by missing values   50
  grouping and sorting   49
  with missing values   50
  without summarizing   47

H

HAVING clause   13
  aggregate functions with   53
  filtering grouped data   51
  filtering grouped data, versus WHERE clause   52
hierarchical data
  expanding in tables   155
host-variable references   128

I

in-line views   108
  temporary tables versus   117
IN operator
  multiple-value subqueries and   75
  retrieving rows   35
indexes   102
  composite   102
  creating   102
  creating with CREATE INDEX statement   102
  deleting   103
  query performance and   116
  tips for creating   102
  unique values   102
informats
  changing column informat   100
INNER JOIN keywords   59
inner joins   57
  comparison operators for   59
  creating with INNER JOIN keywords   59
  data from multiple tables   63
  multicolumn joins   62
  null values and   60
  order of output   59
  reflexive joins   64
  self-joins   64
  showing relationships within a table   64
  table aliases   58
INOBS= option
  restricting row processing   112
inserting rows   93
  with queries   95
  with SET clause   93
  with VALUES clause   94
integrity constraints   103
  referential   104
INTERSECT operator
  combining queries   81, 84
IS MISSING operator
  retrieving rows   36

IS NOT MISSING operator
  inner joins 61
iterations
  limiting 113

J

joins 56
  Cartesian product 57
  COALESCE function in 70
  combining with subqueries 79
  comparing match-merges with 71
  comparing with subqueries 117
  cross joins 68
  inner joins 57
  natural joins 69
  outer joins 65
  reducing size of results 117
  specialty joins 68
  union joins 69
  when to use 80
  WHERE expressions with 117

L

labels
  changing column labels 100
left outer joins 65
libname engines
  querying DBMS tables 138
LIBNAME statement
  connecting to a DBMS 138
libnames
  embedding in views 107
LIKE operator
  retrieving rows 37
logical operators
  retrieving rows 33
LOOPS= option
  limiting iterations 113

M

macro facility
  SQL procedure with 128
macro variables 128
  concatenating values in 130
  creating and using 167
  creating from aggregate function results 129
  creating from query results 128
  creating in SQL procedure 128
  creating multiple 129
  set by SQL procedure 133
macros
  defining to create tables 131
match-merges 71
  comparing with joins 71
  when all values match 71
  when position of values is important 73
  when some values match 72
MEAN function
  summarizing data 41
  WHERE clause with 41
merging
  disabling remerge 120
  remerging summary statistics 42

missing values 3
  finding errors caused by 46
  finding grouping errors caused by 50
  grouping data with 50
  overlaying 150
  replacing in columns 24
  retrieving rows and 36
  sorting columns with 30
  summarizing data with 45
  WHERE clause with 38
multicolumn joins 62
multiple-value subqueries 75

N

natural joins 69
nested subqueries 78
NOEXEC option
  syntax checking with 113
NOT IN operator
  multiple-value subqueries and 75
null values 3
  inner joins and 60

O

observations
  See rows
ODS destinations 142
ODS (Output Delivery System)
  SQL procedure with 142
ORDER BY clause 13
  omitting 117
  query performance and 117
outer joins 65
  full outer joins 67
  including nonmatching rows 65, 66
  left outer joins 65
  right outer joins 66
OUTER UNION operator
  combining queries 81
  concatenating query results 85
OUTOBS= option
  restricting row processing 112
output
  adding text to 18
  formatting with REPORT procedure 136
output objects 142
overlaying missing values 150

P

percentages
  computing within subtotals 152
performance
  queries 116
primary key 104
PROC SQL views
  See also views
  updating 142
PUT function
  deploying inside Teradata 119
  optimizing 118
  reducing 118

Q

qualifying column names 58
queries 2
  adding text to output 18
  ALL keyword in set operations 117
  breaking into steps 117
  combining with set operators 81
  comparing execution time of two queries 114
  creating 112
  DBMS tables 138
  debugging 112
  duplicate rows and performance 117
  in-line views 108
  in-line views versus temporary tables 117
  indexes and 116
  inserting rows with 95
  limiting iterations 113
  performance improvement 116
  restricting row processing 112
  subqueries 74
  validating 53
query results 2
  concatenating 85
  creating macro variables from 128
  creating tables from 91
  deleting duplicate rows 16

R

records
  See rows
referential integrity constraints 104
reflexive joins 64
relational theory 1
relations 1
remerging summary statistics 42
  disabling remerge 120
renaming columns 100
REPORT procedure
  formatting SQL output 136
reports
  creating summary reports 158
RESET statement
  resetting SQL procedure options 115
resetting options 115
retrieving rows 31
  based on comparison 32
  identifying columns with missing values 36
  rows that satisfy a condition 31
  satisfying multiple conditions 33
  with a WHERE clause with missing values 38
  with BETWEEN-AND operators 36
  with IN operator 35
  with IS MISSING operator 36
  with LIKE operator 37
  with other conditional operators 34
  with simple WHERE clause 31
  with truncated string comparison operators 38
return codes
  Pass-Through Facility 141
right outer joins 66
rows 2
  See also retrieving rows
  combining data from multiple rows into single row 42
  counting 45

counting duplicates 153
deleting 98
deleting duplicates 16
duplicates 117
including all 69
including all combinations of 68
inserting 93
inserting with queries 95
inserting with SET clause 93
inserting with VALUES clause 94
matching 69
nonmatching 65, 66
producing from first or second query 86
restricting row processing 112
selecting all 67
updating all rows with same expression 96
updating rows with different expressions 97

S

SAS/ACCESS
  accessing a DBMS 137
SAS/ACCESS LIBNAME statement 137
SAS/ACCESS views
  updating 142
SAS data files
  See tables
SAS data views
  DICTIONARY tables 120
  SAS System information 120
  SASHELP views 120
  retrieving information about 122
SELECT * statement
  expanding with FEEDBACK option 113
SELECT clause 12
SELECT statement 12
  See also WHERE clause
  FROM clause 12
  GROUP BY clause 13
  HAVING clause 13
  ORDER BY clause 13
  ordering clauses 14
  SELECT clause 12
self-joins 64
SET clause
  inserting rows with 93
set operators
  ALL keyword 117
  combining queries with 81
single-value subqueries 75
sort order 25, 27
  customized 161
sorting data 25
  by calculated column 28
  by column 26
  by column position 29
  by multiple columns 26
  by unselected columns 29
  columns with missing values 30
  grouping and sorting 49
sorting sequence 30
SQL 1
SQL procedure 1
  compared with DATA step 3
  creating macro variables 128
  creating queries 112

cumulative time for   114
data set options with   127
debugging queries   112
DICTIONARY tables   120
example tables   5
formatting output   136
macro facility with   128
macro variables set by   133
ODS with   142
resetting options   115
syntax checking   113
terminology   2
timing individual statements   114
using tables in other procedures   170
SQL Procedure Pass-Through Facility   140
connecting to a DBMS   140
example   141
return codes   141
SQLEXITCODE macro variable   133
SQLOBS macro variable   133
SQLOOPS macro variable   113, 133
SQLRC macro variable   134
SQLXMSG macro variable   134
SQLXRC macro variable   135
statistical summaries   40
STIMER option
timing SQL procedure   114
Structured Query Language
See SQL
subqueries   74
combining with joins   79
comparing with joins   117
correlated subqueries   76
multiple nesting levels   78
multiple-value   75
single-value   75
testing for existence of a group of values   77
when to use   80
subtotals
computing percentages within   152
SUM function
summarizing data   42
summarizing data   40
aggregate functions   40
aggregate functions, using   40
aggregate functions with unique values   44
combining data from multiple rows into single row   42
displaying sums   42
in multiple columns   157
remerging summary statistics   42
with missing values   45
with WHERE clause   41
summary functions
See also aggregate functions
disabling remerging of data   120
summary reports
creating   158
summary statistics
remerging   42
sums
displaying   42
syntax checking   113

T

table aliases
abbreviating column names   58
inner joins   58
tables   2
Cartesian product   57
comparing   148
copying   93
counting duplicate rows   153
creating   90
creating, like an existing table   92
creating from column definitions   90
creating from query results   91
creating with data set options   93
creating with macros   131
creating without rows   90
DBMS tables   2
deleting   103
example tables   5
expanding hierarchical data   155
inserting rows   93
integrity constraints   103
joining a table to itself   64
omitting ORDER BY clause when creating   117
selecting all columns   14
selecting columns   14
selecting specific columns   15
SQL tables in other procedures   170
SQL tables in SAS   103
structure of   17
temporary tables versus in-line views   117
update errors   98
updating all rows with same expression   96
updating conditionally   163
updating rows with different expressions   97
updating values   96
updating with values from another table   165
temporary tables
in-line views versus   117
Teradata
deploying PUT function and SAS formats   119
terminology   2
text
adding to output   18
TIME function
replacing references to   119
timing procedure statements   114
TODAY function
replacing references to   119
truncated string comparison operators   38

U

union joins   69
UNION operator
combining queries   81, 82
UNIQUE keyword   102
unique values
aggregate functions with   44
counting   44
counting all rows   45
counting nonmissing values   45
in columns   16
updating tables
conditionally   163

errors   98
    updating values   96
    with values from another table   165
updating views   107, 142
user-defined macro variables   128

V

VALIDATE statement
    syntax checking with   113
validating queries   53
VALUES clause
    inserting rows with   94
variables
    See columns
views   3, 106
    creating   106
    deleting   108
    describing   107
    DICTIONARY tables and   120
    embedding libnames in   107
    in-line   108

of DBMS tables   139
    omitting ORDER BY clause when creating   117
    PROC SQL views in SAS   110
    SAS data views   120
    SASHELP views   120, 122
    tips for using   109
    updating   107
    updating PROC SQL and SAS/ACCESS views   142

W

weighted averages   146
WHERE clause   13
    filtering grouped data, versus HAVING clause   52
    MEAN function with   41
    missing values with   38
    retrieving rows conditionally   31
    summarizing data   41
WHERE expressions
    joins with   117
width
    changing column width   100

Your Turn

We welcome your feedback.

- ☐ If you have comments about this book, please send them to **yourturn@sas.com**. Include the full title and page numbers (if applicable).
- ☐ If you have comments about the software, please send them to **suggest@sas.com**.

Made in the USA
Lexington, KY
07 April 2011